There are far too few voices that spea [...] methodology and mission. This work b [...] festo designed to speak into that merging confluence with passion and instruction. For those who come pre-persuaded to the value of the mission of coaching, this book will sharpen and inspire. For those more skeptical, ready if you dare—you won't maintain your reluctance.

Jeff Christopherson, vice president of the Send Network, North American Mission Board and author of *Kingdom Matrix*

Many will enter the kingdom of heaven because the guy that planted the church that reached them didn't give up—even though he wanted to. Many church planters decide not to give up because of critical coaching conversations that happen with Dino and his tribe. No one is more qualified to write this book!

Clint Clifton, DC/Baltimore Send Missionary, director of New City Network

I have been a fan of Dino's for years. I've often said he's one of the best-kept secrets in the church leadership world. *Sending Well* demonstrates the truth of my belief. It draws out the plans and tools he has used to successfully coach and influence so many planters and leaders.

Artie Davis, lead pastor, Cornerstone Church, Orangeburg, South Carolina

Dino Senesi has a gift for coaching church planters and for creating the platform and training needed for others to coach them. I am grateful for how he has enhanced and improved the coaching we give to Southern Baptist church planters. This book encapsulates what he has learned and shares how others can come alongside and help church planters grow into strong leaders who will be part of transforming our world for Christ. May their numbers be greatly multiplied!

Kevin Ezell, president, North American Mission Board, SBC

From my perspective, Dino Senesi is the right person to write a book on coaching church planters and ministry leaders because he coached me. I benefited greatly from his questions, his investment, and his care for my soul. I am excited about the kingdom impact from this book.

Eric Geiger, vice president of LifeWay Christian Resources

Learning how to coach, in contrast to counseling and mentoring, has been one of the greatest leadership lessons of my life. In *Sending Well*, Dino masterfully presents a comprehensive guide to coaching that I will be referencing and referring to in the years to come. Dino is the man when it comes to coaching!

Daniel Im, director of Church Multiplication for
NewChurches.com, and author of
No Silver Bullets and *Planting Missional Churches*

Sending Well is a must read for anyone who wants to help others grow in their leadership. Dino's practical approach makes coaching feel simple and achievable. He gives tools, tips, and techniques that will unquestionably increase your impact on those you coach.

Mac Lake, senior director of assessment
and development, North American Mission Board

In *Sending Well*, Dino Senesi zeroes in on the crucial issue of how to deliver quality coaching for church planters in North America. Dino has grown deeply in his understanding of both church planting and coaching in the many years I have known him. He knows what he's talking about. If you want to learn how to create and deliver a sustainable and scalable movement of coaching for planters in your organization, this book provides you with the blueprint. It's a privilege to recommend this book, and I am confident it will be a blessing to many.

Robert E. Logan, author of *The Missional Journey*
and *The Discipleship Difference*

More voices compete for a church planter's attention than ever before, and that makes *Sending Well* weighty. In the years I've known Dino, I've never met anyone with a bigger "coaching" heart. If our aim is gospel saturation, we require a healthier, high-capacity pipeline to multiply coaches driven by more than "successful" church planters and churches. *Sending Well* is a needed fuel for that pipeline!

Neal McGlohon, lead visionary of The Cypress Project

The church planter coaching relationship is vital to ensuring well-supported planters and healthy churches. Importantly, Dino focuses on the coach. This is a must-read book. Dino brings his many years of experience in coaching, developing coaches, and building coaching frameworks that clarify the key ingredients to providing a strong coaching system.

Scott Sanders, executive director of Geneva Push

I've relied on Dino's wisdom for decades, and now you can as well. Dino is a coach of coaches, and this field guide will help you be the coach your church planter needs.

Ed Stetzer, Billy Graham Distinguished Chair, Wheaton College

Through an easy-to-use framework, *Sending Well* equips coaches with biblical principles, practical questions, and passionate care for church planters. Anyone in ministry would benefit from reading and applying the practical and biblical coaching methods in this book.

Keith E. Webb, author of *The COACH Model for Christian Leaders*

SENDING WELL

SENDING WELL

A FIELD GUIDE TO GREAT CHURCH PLANTER COACHING

DINO SENESI

NASHVILLE, TENNESSEE

978-1-4627-5124-2

Published by B&H Publishing Group
Nashville, Tennessee

Dewey Decimal Classification: 254.1
Subject Heading: CHURCH PLANTING—HANDBOOKS,
MANUALS, ETC. \ CHURCH PLANTING—STUDY AND
TEACHING

1 2 3 4 5 6 • 21 20 19 18 17

Dedication

"Team,

While listening to our call this morning I was reminded of how important it is to establish relationships with these new planters. Some of these men have completely uprooted their lives in order to serve in a community that they have no knowledge of. They have taken their children out of schools trusting that God will be provisional with them. They have left their jobs and a blanket of security to serve the kingdom, and we can play a pivotal role in their lives."

Dwayne Simmons, Cleveland Coaching Champion
To: Send Cleveland Church Planter Coaches
April 29, 2016

This book is dedicated to church planters, their families, and the coaches who walk beside them.

Contents

Foreword

Coaching makes me think of sports. As long as I can remember, coaching has been a part of my life. I played every sport my parents would allow and many coaches helped me along the way. I had some good coaches and a few bad coaches. I even had some coaches who were just other kid's dads who wanted to ensure that their son got the ball. Now, in my thirties, I coach baseball and football and I love it. Coaching has been a consistent theme in my life—one that has carried over into my work in the church.

As a twenty-five-year-old with a degree in marketing and three hours of seminary credit (I eventually finished), I set out to plant a church in a city that I really didn't like, with a group of people who I thought might not last long (many didn't) and the pastoral experience of a ministry intern. My lack of experience was compounded by the fact that I did not have a sending church or anyone to coach me through the process of church planting. I simply showed up in the city one day wondering what in the world I was supposed to do next. I started by meeting with other local pastors and community leaders who asked me one consistent question: *Who is coaching you through this process?* It must have been pretty obvious to them I needed someone to coach me through the perilous challenges that face church planters.

Finally, I asked a ministry leader in the city if he would coach me and he said, "No." I get it, I was a failure waiting to happen and who wants to coach the guy who doesn't appear to have the experience to make it happen? I continued to pester this guy and another local pastor near the city until they both referred me to Dino Senesi.

Two days later I sat at a sandwich shop talking to Dino and asked him if he would coach me, all the while expecting the familiar "No" that I had already heard from others. To my surprise, he said "Yea, let's give it a try." I had no idea what the Lord was blessing me with that day and I am not sure if Dino knew what he was getting himself into either.

The Lord knew I would need someone like Dino. Before we ever launched the church plant, two of my best friends and key leaders in the church sat me down and said they were quitting because they didn't agree with the vision of the church and that they didn't trust me as a leader. During that same period, two core team members who were dating decided to move in together and others scheduled meetings with me to break-up with me, and with the church. The "it's not you, it's me" line was quickly getting old. When I thought things could get no worse, a ministry leader in the area called numerous pastors and denominational leaders and told them not to support what I was doing because the church was destined to fail.

Two of my best friends quit, I had to walk through a church discipline issue, core group members were leaving left and right, and the little support I had from other churches was on the brink of ending. And that was all before the church launched. By the way, if you are reading this book and happen to be considering church planting, keep reading. I promise, it does get better.

Enter Dino. I had no idea how to reconcile all that was occurring but now I had a coach. I would have quit if God had not put a coach in my life in that moment. I will never forget the day after all of this came to a head as I sat across the room from Dino. There was a lot he could have said and if he were a consultant there's probably a good bit of strategy and advice he would have given me. But he was not a consultant; he was a coach. He wasn't primarily intent on refining my skills; He wanted to see God shape my heart. He pointed me back to my original calling to plant a gospel-centered church that would live out God's mission in the city. He looked at me and said, "What do you pray that God will do in this city?" Dino's questions were the result of prayer and preparation and God used them to profoundly shape my life. His coaching was life-giving and life-changing. Dino spoke directly to the calling God had put on my heart and then followed it up with strong questions like . . .

"What are you going to do about it?"
"What's your next step?"
"Who else do you need to talk with?"
"When will you have this complete by?"
"How can I help?"

Dino was qualified, prepared, and inspired by the Holy Spirit to give me clear insight into my work as a church planter. As you read this book, seek out the qualifications that will allow you to learn the proficiencies of a coach so that you can serve others the way Dino served me.

As Dino makes clear, coaching is not some "fly by the seat of your pants" endeavor, but rather a set of abilities that can be learned and developed. The church planters who are on the front lines of mission desperately need prepared and caring coaches who can guide them in God's mission.

I would have bowed out of the church planting game in October of 2006 but, by God's grace, I had a coach like Dino to guide me. In His time the Lord blessed and did allow us to plant a healthy church that is now multiplying disciples and planting gospel-centered churches who are living out God's mission. This is what I dreamed of when we first started and what Dino continued to push me toward all along.

One of the greatest coaches of all time, John Wooden, said, "A good coach can change a game. A great coach can change a life."[1] I have had many coaches who helped change a moment or a situation for me, but God used Dino Senesi to change my life. I believe this book will be transformational to you and will help you understand what it means to have a heart for "Sending Well".

Dustin Willis, church planter,
Midtown Fellowship, Columbia, South Carolina
author of *The Simplest Way to Change the World*,
Life on Mission, and *Life in Community*

Introduction

"Do you think coaching will be around a few years from now, or will it be just another one of those things?" A close friend of mine was not challenging me; he was asking a legitimate question. I thought a minute and gave him as honest an answer as I could: "For some of us, yes; for others, no. Some of us need more coaching than others."

I am one of those people who needs more coaching. For more than fifteen years I have been on the coaching bandwagon. I have spent hours training and being trained. I have spent even more hours coaching and being coached. In the process, I have seen God use coaching to help leaders gain focus, solve problems, and get results. Here are three reasons why I will coach and be coached for the rest of my life.

Three Reasons Coaching Will Stick Around

1. Coaching supports a relational model for discipleship.

Paul spoke of his discipling relationships warmly: "So, being affectionately desirous of you, we were ready to share with you not only the gospel of God but also our own selves, because you had become very dear to us" (1 Thess. 2:8).

At times we are guilty of a "be well, be fed" approach to church planters. We ask planter candidates questions about conversion, calling, behaviors, and a few about character. Then we lay hands on them, pray, and wish them the best. *But who is engaging in consistent, personal conversations with the people God is sending to plant churches?*

1

Coaches go to deep places in the lives of missionary-planters. They engage the unique stories of each planter, learning about plans, dreams, and disappointments, and help connect planters' stories with God's bigger story. *Ultimately, coaching is a relationship between two disciples.*

2. Coaching creates a platform for leadership development.

Everybody's not the same, so they don't respond to the same leadership approaches. Leading leaders is different from leading followers. We need this reminder often: some of the people we lead are leaders, just like us. The Golden Rule of Leadership Development is *lead as you want to be led.*

> Who is engaging in consistent, personal conversations with the people God is sending to plant churches?

High-level leaders need space to process, experiment, and make discoveries on their own. Did you notice how Jesus developed His first twelve leaders? He sent them quickly, but He stayed connected relationally. In the process, He asked great questions as He helped them debrief, grow, and discover His ways.

3. Coaching counters a one-size-fits-all mentality for God's mission.

A church planter whom God has called is doing something never done before. Never in history has a person planted a church in their exact location, at their exact time, with their specific combination of gifts, with their particular people. Are there some one-size-fits-all principles and practices that will help? Absolutely. But if that were all it took, no church planter would ever fail! Hearing God, discovering next steps, and being accountable are parts of any formula, even a time-tested one.

Sending Well

Jesus told His disciples, "As the Father has sent me, even so I am sending you" (John 20:21). We are commonly inspired by Jesus' words to send more. That's a good thing. But His words also speak to the way we send—we must embrace the importance of sending *well*. Did the Father send well? Yes! A great church planter coach co-operates with the Father to send well.

Sending well is a hands-on enterprise. In Acts 13, Paul and Barnabas were sent by the leadership of a local church in Antioch. Upon further review, we discover a high level of intentionality among the Antioch church leaders. Worshiping, praying, and fasting were parts of the sending party. Sending was God's work, but they were comfortable in their role as co-senders.

Everyone was fully engaged in the sending. Ownership was strong with both the senders (Simeon, Lucius, Manaen) and the sent (Paul, Barnabas). Two high-level members of Antioch were liberated to go on the ultimate business trip: God's mission.

The ultimate business trip was historic. The risk was incredible. The results were not guaranteed. Sending got the fullest attention of everyone involved. Coaching is about sending and sending well. Every detail is important, and every missionary needs our best support.

Obsess over the Target

Thriving church planter coaching relationships are happening now, but the stakes have been raised. A new goal has been defined: making church planter coaching available to everyone who plants a church in North America. This is a daunting task. I began to pursue this goal by asking church planting leaders in different contexts the same questions and listening to their answers. For example:

- What is the history of coach training in your area?
- What are the critical qualifications of a church planter coach?
- What is currently happening with church planter coaching?

Though I didn't discover a magic bullet for church planter coaching success, I gained clarity regarding the problem we needed to solve.

I learned that the problem was not:

- *Belief in the value of coaching*—Every leader I talked with acknowledged more and better church planter coaching was desperately needed.
- *Quality coach training*—Coaches had experienced strong coach training through CoachNet, Gospel Coach, Redeemer City to City, and Coaching Qualification Training from my mission organization—the North American Mission Board.
- *A shortage of coaches*—Most planters already had someone they considered their coach.

Though the above were not major problems, I discovered significant challenges:

- *Lack of capacity*—Though most church planting leaders supported coaching, they did not have the time required to oversee a coaching delivery system.
- *Lack of clarity*—Each person I spoke with had a definition of coaching. However, a consistent definition of church planter coaching did not emerge from my conversations. Whose coaching philosophy is right or wrong was not the issue. But to create a coaching system that will scale (grow to meet the demand) and sustain (endure over time), leaders must agree on what kind of coaching planters will receive.
- *Lack of consistency*—Practical coaching approaches ranged from a new planter living in the same home with an experienced, successful church planter to a few random coffee shop conversations a year. Some planters were getting the best, and others were getting random leftovers from random leaders.

Meeting the Need

I received a gift from the hours spent studying survey data and having individual conversations with church planting leaders. And that gift is a question: *How can we consistently deliver great church planter coaching to every church planter in North America?*

Sending Well: A Field Guide for Great Church Planter Coaching is an effort to help answer that question. High-quality coach training systems exist, but training is only one aspect of delivery. Delivery is a more challenging target.

Below are the three parts of *Sending Well*:

> How can we consistently deliver great church planter coaching to every church planter in North America?

Part One: Build a Coaching Framework

For a system to work, everybody needs to understand the "Why?" "How?" "What?" and "Who?" When the coach, the planter, church planting leaders, and sending churches look to the future, all must see the same picture.

Part Two: Develop Great Coaches

Great coaches are made, not born. The "great" target means all of us see the preferred future, but we are not there yet. The "10 Qualities of a Great Coach" creates simple developmental targets for coaches. Coaches will always coach before they're ready. But our systems need to provide on-the-job training and further development.

Part Three: Deliver Great Coaching

A delivery obsession made one small pizza store in Michigan called DomiNick's into a multimillion-dollar industry called Domino's. We are obsessed as well. And the right environment is the pathway. "Obsess over Delivery," "Value Sending Churches," "Create a Coaching Culture," and "Practice Church Planter Coaching" are all keys to scalability and sustainability.

Like a washing machine, the cycle below must spin continuously to produce the desired outcome of the Sending Well Field Guide:

A church planter coaching system fueled by great coaches who deliver great coaching to every church planter.

PART 1

Build a Coaching Platform

Coaching helps church planters pursue their unique kingdom assignment.

Giuseppe Senesi was an Italian immigrant who lived in Pennsylvania during the 1930s. He worked hard in the coal mines to provide for his family, and he paid the ultimate price for his work.

Returning to Italy in 1939 in hopes of regaining his health, Giuseppe died from coal miners' asthma that same year. His son, who was seven years old at the time, went to work setting pins in a bowling alley to support his mother, Rose, and his sister, Maryann.

As a third grader, my father (Giuseppe's son) would come home from work at midnight, often leaving chocolate candy on his little sister's bedside table. Then, he would put himself to bed to get up early the next morning for school.

He never wanted my life to resemble his, and it hasn't. Knowing my father's story gives me a valuable perspective on his generosity. He was determined to make my life better than his.

He bought me my first car, a used, royal blue, 1971 Volkswagen Super Beetle. My car was nicer than the cars most of my friends drove, a meaningful gift from my generous father.

I am clueless as to where the old, custom-painted Super Beetle is today. Maybe it's a reconditioned classic in someone's garage, but I doubt it. More likely, it is resting in rusty pieces at an East Tennessee junkyard. What I do know is that I loved the car, and it got me to places I needed to go. Places like Hampton High School, baseball practice, and an occasional date.

The vehicle is a vivid memory from my teenage years. I wish I had a picture of myself standing beside it, but I don't. In the grand scheme of things, my Volkswagen was merely an insignificant detail, something that got me from here to there for a season.

Your Unique Kingdom Assignment

Coaching, like my Volkswagen, is a vehicle to help people get from here to there for a season. Coaching is a gift that some of us have enjoyed both giving and receiving. But the real coaching story is not about the gift; it's about the Giver. In simple terms, the ways we live and serve are what obedience looks like in our lives when Jesus—the Giver—has His way.

For some people, obedience may be a life surrendered to helping the poor. Helping the poor is their "How?"[1] of kingdom life. Others may spend all their discretionary time with teenagers or college students, or in helping people during times of personal crisis. In our context, the "How?" is church planting.

The Coaching Platform helped me gain a new perspective on how coaches and coaching fit into God's big picture. As a result, the weight of our efforts to live the way God intended us to live and serve the way God intended us to serve dramatically increased. And the significance (as well as the insignificance) of coaching was clarified for me: *Coaching helps church planters pursue their unique kingdom assignment.*

> Coaching helps church planters pursue their unique kingdom assignment.

For a church planter *coach*, the "How?" of kingdom life is coaching. Coaching is merely a vehicle being used at the moment to help a planter pursue his unique kingdom assignment. The church planter coach humbly and passionately accepts his role providing support, encouragement, and accountability.

**Coaching helps church planters pursue
their unique kingdom assignment**

People discover their "How?" at different times in their lives. But no matter how young or old someone is when they discover their "How?"—or if it changes over a lifetime—at the moment, the whole world revolves around their discovery.

God's people operate in obedience to God's assignment at the moment. Moses was caring for his father-in-law's sheep in the desert when obedience changed for him. With his co-leader Aaron, Moses' flock changed from sheep to people.

Paul and Barnabas were on the leadership team at a church in Antioch when obedience changed for them. Sent out on a new missionary endeavor, both Paul and Barnabas had a new and unique assignment.

The passion of the Christian movement rests in the unique ways God asks us to live for Him. This passion is a gift from our incredibly generous heavenly Father.

The Body of Christ

Your passion may revolve around coaching, church planting, marginalized people, or international students. But regardless of the "How?" for this season of your life, the eternal significance is preeminent. The "Why?" is the kingdom. The "What?" is the King's glory and the King's message—the gospel.

The beauty of the body of Christ is in full view. We are all in the same business, passionate about the same outcomes—yet in diverse ways. These diverse ways describe our unique kingdom assignments.

- Coaching is a *vehicle* (How?)
- To *help* church planters (Who?)
- *Pursue* their unique kingdom assignment (Why?)
- *For the* King's glory and *the* King's message—the gospel (What?)

Through a biblical lens God's values become prominent. Kingdom citizens live for the King's pleasure and serve for His glory.

"But seek first the kingdom of God and his righteousness, and all these things will be added to you." (Matt. 6:33)

For I am not ashamed of the gospel, for it is the power of God for salvation to everyone who believes, to the Jew first and also to the Greek. (Rom. 1:16)

For just as the body is one and has many members, and all the members of the body, though many, are one body, so it is with Christ. (1 Cor. 12:12)

Coaching helps church planters pursue their unique kingdom assignment. Church planter coaches and the planters they coach must see the same picture of the future. Building a Coaching Platform helps ensure this will be the case. Part 1 of *Sending Well* describes the four elements of building a coaching platform: Kingdom; Planters; Coaches; Coaching.

CHAPTER 1

Advance Kingdom Values

Synchronized swimming has always entertained me. The Olympic sport attempts to synchronize the detailed movements of water ballet dancers. Years of training and commitment are required for success in such a precise sport.

The first public presentation of water ballet happened in 1907 and evolved into a competitive sport soon afterward. The 1984 Olympic Games in Los Angeles hosted synchronized swimming as a medal sport for the first time.[1] I find the robotic movements of these athletes comical, I confess. But I am amazed at the perfection and discipline required to excel. If life were only as beautiful and perfect as synchronized swimming, the world would be a better place.

Unique Kingdom Assignments

Synchronized church planting would hold great promise, too, if it were only possible. The next one hundred planters could jump into the planting pool at the same time, master the same movements, and earn gold medals in their respective communities.

But every kingdom assignment is unique. A new church is a one-time-in-history endeavor. If we expect to reach the diverse peoples of North America with the gospel, synchronized church planting cannot be our method.

How is each church planting assignment unique? Here are five once-in-history circumstances every planter faces:

1. The Place

Will Mancini calls place the "Local Predicament" in his book, *Church Unique*. The Local Predicament is "about having an intimate grasp of the soil where God has called you to minister."[2] Place is the primary part of a planter's assignment. My friend, Neal McGlohon, issues a challenge to planters in The Cypress Project (http://cypressproject.org/): "Do you love your city so much that if your church plant fails you will stay there anyway?"

Demographics, spiritual history, moral history, subcultures, and geography are only a few layers of influence in any particular place. Adding to the cultural complexity is the reality that each of these layers is constantly evolving at different rates. So what is true about a place today could change six months from now.

2. The Planter

Place is not the only multilayered complexity. The church planter has his own layers, such as spiritual gifts, natural strengths, ethnicity, ministry experiences, family history, church background, past pain, past failures, emotional maturity, etc. And, like place, all the planter's layers are evolving in the moment.

3. The Plan

Planters typically come with vision, passion, and strategies. Church planting models vary from attractional methods to more community-based house churches. The plan will evolve with constant updates, revisions, and makeovers as the understanding of the place, planter, people, and purpose matures. Another reason for the evolution is that God is shaping His church and disciples into His image.

4. The People

The "crowd" that is comprised of the core team, lead team, sending church, mentors, coaches, advisors, etc., is a unique collection of people. These crowds have unique backgrounds, passions, and opinions about the way things ought to be. No two planting teams will ever be the same.

5. The Purpose

Although a church planter must cast a clear vision for his team, the "Why are we here?" and "What does God want?" questions are always under consideration. These questions feel like moving targets, even to an experienced planter. The team's vision will be challenged by day-to-day ministry pressures and by people with many different ideas of what should be done.

Church planters could fully prepare in a classroom if all situations were identical, but as we have discovered, they are not. While classroom preparation is an important part of the equipping process, the dynamic nature of the task demands a more customized approach. The role of coaches is to help planters pursue the ongoing challenges of their assignment in real time after the classroom preparation has ended.

The King Assigns

Obedience to our King is the aim of kingdom citizens. The outcome of our obedience is the King's glory and the extension of gospel influence to all peoples. If we don't start here, we become an industry or institution rather than part of a movement of God. A church planting system then becomes a faithless, lifeless, uninspired assembly line of product development and delivery.

> Obedience to our King is the aim of kingdom citizens.

The entire church planting process (assessment, training, coaching, and planter care) is highly relational. Church planting communities are partners in the gospel helping each other live a life of obedience to our King. So even the painstaking obligations and details of the process are all for a greater purpose: all we do, however trivial it may seem, is "for the Lord." Paul reminds believers:

Whatever you do, work heartily, as for the Lord and not for men. (Col. 3:23)

What happens when two disciples of Jesus get together to discuss personal obedience? Jesus speaks into the conversation. And when the King speaks, everything changes.

My close friend, expert coach, and coach developer, Eddie Hancock, describes the coaching moment in a memorable way: "We incline our ears together to listen to the Holy Spirit." We crave moments like these in the presence of our King.

What You Don't Need to Know about the Kingdom

Listen to Jesus as He taught about the kingdom of God in order to prepare His disciples for the future:

He presented himself alive to them after his suffering by many proofs, appearing to them during forty days and speaking about the kingdom of God. (Acts 1:3)

Jesus addressed the topic—the kingdom—most relevant to His students and the movement.

One of my favorite coaching questions is, "What is your biggest question?" The "biggest question" question helps people work through their distractions and ask the most relevant question in the moment. Coaches realize that most of the time, the biggest question is already inside the planter; he just needs help identifying it.

What was the disciples' biggest question?

So when they had come together, they asked him, "Lord, will you at this time restore the kingdom to Israel?" He said to them, "It is not for you to know times or seasons that the Father has fixed by his own authority." (Acts 1:6–7)

Imagine watching the amazing Jesus preach, teach, heal, and cast out demons for three years. Many of the people who had been transformed by Jesus' power were determined to crown Him king. If a temporary kingdom was Jesus' mission, He would have let them coronate Him; He could have successfully built an earthly kingdom.

Jesus represented the ordinary fishermen, tax collectors, and prostitutes. The Messiah who would free the people from their religious and governmental oppression was here, and He was here now. Witnessing His brutal crucifixion and miraculous resurrection brought even greater hope. If Jesus could defeat death, what earthly kingdom could stop Him?

Rather than granting their requests for an earthly kingdom, Jesus taught about His eternal kingdom; but they couldn't grasp it. He corrected their focus on themselves, their needs, and their goals. "It is not for you to know . . ." (Acts 1:7). Jesus answered their biggest question about the restoration of His kingdom—but not in the way they hoped.

What You Need to Know about the Kingdom

When His students asked about the kingdom of Israel, Jesus answered with a powerful prediction about the kingdom of God:

> "But you will receive power when the Holy Spirit has come upon you, and you will be my witnesses in Jerusalem and in all Judea and Samaria, and to the end of the earth." (Acts 1:8)

What do we need to know about God's kingdom? Consider these five characteristics:

1. The kingdom will move outward quickly in multiple directions.

The power of the gospel will produce an inexplicable outward explosion of missionary personnel. One young lady will hear God's call to Nigeria and spend her life caring for orphans who need to know Jesus. Another man will be passionate about homeless people sleeping under a bridge in his hometown. A young family will leave well-paying jobs and great schools to move to Vancouver to plant a church.

This kingdom impulse pushes people outward, everywhere, with intense urgency. Geographic boundaries cannot stop them. People respond to the King's message and then move in different directions. Every direction matters to God. In the kingdom, all citizens who obey God's voice and run with passion are loved by the King equally.

2. The kingdom will shatter social, political, cultural, spiritual, and geographic barriers.

Clashing worldviews of believers and nonbelievers from different backgrounds pose barriers to kingdom advancement. But God's kingdom agenda is not to upgrade existing systems; the kingdom replaces them. Too many believers are hoping for a better version of what they have. A different president, a "more Christian" culture, less violence, or better government programs could relieve symptoms for a moment. But like an old car that has taken one too many trips to the mechanic, a replacement is the only permanent solution. Jesus' birth announcement predicted: "'And he will reign over Israel forever; his Kingdom will never end!'" (Luke 1:33 NLT).

3. Kingdom citizens will be empowered and equipped by the Holy Spirit.

Where will we get the money? How will we train the people? How will we overcome the physical threats? How will we reach the religious and the irreligious? How will we communicate with different people groups? We are not limited to natural resources for these dilemmas; God will give us everything we need to do what He wants.

4. The kingdom will not follow logical patterns of expansion.

"Urgently go everywhere to everyone" seems illogical. The more logical suggestion of "Let's win all the locals first; then they can help us move out from here" was rejected by the King. As you look again, you can see the brilliance of the King's strategy. Everyone who embraces the gospel is immediately a missionary. Jesus instructed kingdom citizens to go to all nations as quickly as possible, win people everywhere, and let them scatter and reach the rest.

5. The kingdom will advance with or without us.

That's a relief, right? Who would not want to be a part of this kind of movement? We see a picture of a sovereign God's expansion plan. This God rules and reigns in the affairs of men. Jesus' words were not a command; they were a prediction. What a humbling thought—God is able do His work without me.

Acts 1:8 presents what Jesus saw in the future; it allows us to see His vision. "Here is what My kingdom will look like," was Jesus' answer. When you see it, join in! And they would see it, sooner than they thought.

The Big Idea

Coaching fruitfulness increases when both coach and planter see the same kingdom picture. The end game is not coaching, nor one great local church; the end game is the kingdom. The coach views himself as part of the sending team. As he coaches, he expands his sending capacity and contributes to the kingdom.

When all of our passion is invested in the expansion of one location, we limit God's plan and our influence. The local church is no more than a dot on the map, and life change is limited to only a few. To view the church as a key outpost to advance the larger kingdom adds great significance. Jeff Christopherson describes the role of the local church in the kingdom of God:

> *Coaching fruitfulness increases when both coach and planter see the same kingdom picture.*

As much as I love the local church, I have to remind myself that the local church was never meant to be the goal. The local body of Christ is a *tool* to advance the Kingdom of

God, not the *goal* of the Kingdom of God. Local churches are temporary; they have a life cycle, a shelf life.[3]

Kingdom values drive effective coaching. Coaching a church planter and caring for his family may not always provide a direct payoff for church-centric thinkers. The value is seldom measurable in those terms.

Multiplying churches and leaders are blessed, but the blessing is in obedience. Biblical motivation supports this focus: "We are willing to die to multiply gospel influence; we gladly surrender our church-centric agenda for His kingdom agenda."

When Jesus prepared His leaders to launch a global movement, He saw something larger than a series of independently owned local *McChurch* franchises. Kingdom coaches become multipliers who see the significance of helping leaders:

Kingdom multipliers love the other laborers as much as laboring.

Kingdom multipliers love the other witnesses as much as witnessing.

Kingdom multipliers love the other disciple makers as much as discipling.

Kingdom multipliers love the other church planters as much as church planting.[4]

If we embrace the reality that the kingdom, not the local church, is the end goal, then we must understand the values of the kingdom. The greatest treasure in the kingdom is the King Himself:

On his robe and on his thigh he has a name written, King of kings and Lord of lords. (Rev. 19:16)

The King, His glory, and His message (the gospel) are preeminent. After the King, kingdom citizens are next highest in value:

But you are a chosen race, a royal priesthood, a holy nation, a people for his own possession, that you may proclaim the excellencies of him who called you out of darkness into his marvelous light. (1 Pet. 2:9)

Being part of a chosen, royal, and holy collection of people who are property of the King is a great position. Kingdom coaches understand this, and they see the planters they coach through a kingdom lens:

1. Every planter is precious to God, as are his family, his core team, and their families.
2. The planter's humanity, spiritual maturity, and emotional maturity will influence church planting outcomes and outlast his church planting strategy.
3. Success is defined by obedience, not quantitative results alone.
4. Planters are responding to God's unique assignment at the moment, but their assignment will likely change in the future.

Coaches Value Obedience

Coaches must encourage planters to obey God in all things. When a planter moves on from planting to a new assignment, many coaches see it as a worst-case scenario. But this means the King has another assignment for this planter. The apparent lack of success does not necessarily make the planter a risk or a failure. Success is measured differently in the kingdom: Obedience = Success

Even if the planter never plants again, his kingdom value has not diminished. A coach withholds judgment of the planter and encourages obedience. A great coach abides with the leader and his family beyond their church plant.

God assigns and reassigns His leaders over the course of a lifetime. How many times has that happened to you? I am currently in my seventh unique kingdom assignment.

During my first assignment in 1983, I was discipled and mentored by Ray Jones, the current worship pastor at Community Bible Church (www.communitybible.com) in San Antonio, Texas. Over thirty-five years of doing life with Ray included celebrations and setbacks, but we have learned to see each other beyond our ministry assignments. Who we are has always been more important than what we do. Ray sees me as a person.

The following are more stories of the King's appointment to various unique kingdom assignments.

Different Kingdom Assignments

Jeff Christopherson

Jeff Christopherson was twenty-two years old when he attempted to plant his first church as a bi-vocational planter working at a furniture store. He had no training, core group, church support, or help. The church did not survive.

The experience was demoralizing. Jeff felt like a failure and doubted his call to ministry. He abandoned any future plans of church planting or ministry. He then read a booklet by Bill Tinsley called "Upon This Rock," which rekindled his faith. Jeff decided to enroll in seminary and prepare for ministry (but not church planting).

Some could have considered Jeff a huge risk to plant again. Yet his value as a kingdom citizen remained. More assignments were coming. Church planting was in his future.

After planting a healthy church in Calgary, Jeff, Laura, and three other families moved to Toronto to plant "The Sanctuary" in 2001. In the church's first year, they baptized fifty-two people. The Sanctuary started nine daughter churches. In addition, they birthed a church planting infrastructure within The Sanctuary, Toronto Church Planting (torontochurchplanting.com), which impacts the Greater Toronto Area today. Currently, Jeff is the vice president of the Send Network, where he leads church planting efforts in North America for the North American Mission Board (NAMB).

Artie Davis

Artie Davis's first church plant was in Clemson, South Carolina. After more than three years of trying to make this church work, Artie gave up, moved to another city, and got a job in the marketplace.

After graduating from Columbia International University in 1990, Artie moved back to the same area and attempted to plant his second church. With no real organized plan or vision, this church plant had identical results to his first one. Artie admitted that he planted with mixed motives but said the plant was "more out of rebellion to traditional church than a call from God."

Artie's third church plant met in a dance studio in Orangeburg, South Carolina. His vision was to plant a multiethnic church in a small, diverse town. After planting two churches that didn't survive, Artie was attempting the impossible in the most difficult location yet. But God didn't see it that way. God was simply reassigning a kingdom citizen.

Cornerstone Church in Orangeburg, South Carolina, is a multiethnic, multisite church that celebrated their twentieth anniversary last year. Cornerstone reaches people with the King's message both locally and globally. Artie influences leaders throughout North America with his vision and passion for planting churches in small towns like Orangeburg. I'm glad Artie kept going.

Ron Renner

Ron Renner planted Gateway Church in Fairfield, Ohio, in 2000. In their three years of existence, they experienced strong kingdom wins including lives changed by the gospel. However, the church did not survive.

Following Gateway Church, Ron spent seven years as a Human Resources Manager at a small company in Cincinnati. A new kingdom assignment was provided miraculously. Ron said, "God used this job as a disguise for ministry." Ron was free to minister on the job, caring, praying, and sharing the gospel.

During this season, Ron stayed connected to two local churches providing transitional pastoral leadership. He also helped church planters as a strategist and a coach. New kingdom assignments were lived out, and more were coming.

Ron is now lead pastor of M2 Multi-Ethnic Ministries of Power Mission Church in Cincinnati. The church focuses developing people to be next-generation leaders. The congregation consists of college students, career professionals, and young married couples of multiple ethnicities. Ron is touching the nations from Cincinnati: a new kingdom assignment.

Kingdom Values

Life did not end for Ron when Gateway Church ceased to exist; in fact, it was only the beginning. The same goes for Jeff and Artie. All of these leaders remained a valuable part of a "chosen race, a royal priesthood, a holy nation, a people for his own possession" (1 Pet. 2:9). New assignments were in the works.

The value of these leaders in God's eyes stayed the same as it had always been, in spite of what many would call failures. A kingdom coach sees a church planter as a precious possession of the King and coaching as a kingdom responsibility. Clint Clifton, Send City Missionary and church planter in Washington, D.C., said, "Churches, just like people, have lifecycles. They are born to die."[5]

The church is a platform to "proclaim the excellencies of Him," not a leadership caste system of successes and failures. Seeds (people) of these churches continue to reproduce and multiply through their unique kingdom assignments. Obedience equals success in the kingdom.

People move to new kingdom assignments, but the kingdom remains in places like Alberta, South Carolina, and Ohio. Neal McGlohon of The Cypress Project once said to me:

We would all prefer to reap, but what if we are "just" part of the sowing in that geography? Do we celebrate the kingdom advancing, even if our church doesn't? What if taking responsibility for lostness in your place costs you success?

Great church planter coaches care about the kingdom more than the local church. The planters they coach are not valued because of what they do, but because of who they are in Christ. The Coaching Platform must, first and foremost, advance kingdom values. When it does so, coaches will withhold judgment, define success as obedience, and remember that more assignments are coming. Be your planter's biggest fan!

Be Coached . . .

1. What was the highlight of this chapter for you?

2. What idea is leading you to act?

3. What are you going to do?

4. When are you going to do it?

My Coach Helps . . .

My coach helps me to keep my priorities straight so I'm able to say yes to the most fundamental things in my ministry. Also, he has taught me a basic structure for coaching others. The coaching experience has given me a rich sense of unity and brotherhood with my fellow workers in the kingdom. It's good to know you're not alone in this endeavor.

Yuri Kreyman
Bethel Community
Aurora, Colorado
www.bethelrussianchurch.org

 **CHAPTER 2**

Help Church Planters

Chariots of Fire is one of the greatest movies in history. Released in 1981, the movie was based on the true story of two Olympic runners—Eric Liddell and Harold Abrahams. Images, stories, and clips from this movie have been included in numerous sermons and books. The scene of the barefoot Olympic runners splashing along a beach with the familiar musical score playing in the background is unforgettable.

Eric Liddell was a Scottish Christian born of missionary parents. In an argument with his sister over her concerns about his waning commitment to God, he famously said:

> I believe that God made me for a purpose. But He also made me fast, and when I run, I feel His pleasure.

In the same conversation, Liddell promised to return to China to be a missionary, which he did. He died there in 1945.[1]

Church planters pursue their unique kingdom assignment with the same passion and commitment. To "pursue" means to chase after something or someone. Most church planters are competitors by nature. They are apostolic, independent, and passionate. In bold faith, they have stepped onto the beach to fulfill God's purpose and experience His pleasure for their lives. A poem by William Blake inspired the title of *Chariots of Fire*. Blake's word picture captures a church planter planter's passion:

Bring me my Bow of burning gold;
Bring me my Arrows of desire:
Bring me my Spear: O clouds unfold!
Bring me my Chariot of fire!
("Jerusalem" by William Blake, 1804)[2]

Coaches Run with Planters

All planters have an identical mission, but no two planters have exactly the same passion. John and Diane Worcester are always on the run. In their amazing pursuit of God's call, they have planted churches in cities like Moscow, Toronto, and Fort Worth. John tells part of their story:

> God has called my wife, Diane, and me to be sequential church planters. We move to one city after another to plant churches. Our goal is to make disciples of unsaved people and gather them in churches, where they can mature and be mobilized to make more disciples. By God's grace, we have planted eight churches and over a dozen other expressions of the church, such as evangelistic campus ministries, singles ministries, etc. We typically apprentice future church planters as we plant, and once the church starts, we turn the church over to a long-term pastor.

As planters like John and Diane Worcester run after what God has called them to do, their coaches run alongside them. God has used them to make an incredible gospel impact for thousands of people. No doubt well-intended advisors suggested they stop moving so often, but God had a unique plan. Paul reminds Thessalonian believers to give honor, respect, and love to those who lead:

> Dear brothers and sisters, honor those who are your leaders in the Lord's work. They work hard among you and give you spiritual guidance. Show them great respect and

wholehearted love because of their work. And live peacefully with each other. (1 Thess. 5:12–13 NLT)

God gives coaches extraordinary relationships with leaders. Coaches see church planters as those leaders in the Lord's work. Age and experience and apparent success are irrelevant—they are our partners in the gospel.

As a coach, a planter's pursuit becomes your pursuit. You are more than a friend or a donor; you love them like God loves you. Review the passage from 1 Thessalonians again, underlining key words and phrases that speak to you. Stop and pray for a planter you are coaching or who is close to you. Encourage them in their pursuit this week.

I Can Help You

My business coach, Glenn Smith, gave me an important tip. When discussing a coaching proposal with a prospective client, he encouraged me to say, "I can help you." I don't know how that looks to you, but I can tell you how it felt the first time I used those words. They terrified me! How do I know that? Did I just commit the unpardonable sin of business—the overpromise?

If we don't believe God can use us to help planters or anyone we coach, we are hypocrites. Why else would we be coaching? Making that promise to potential coaching clients was more important for me to say than for them to hear. The promise reminded me of my purpose. For those I coached, this strengthened my resolve to deliver something worthwhile.

If you can't say with confidence "I can help you" to the next planter you coach, then don't take on the coaching relationship—defer to someone else. Then, pray, get more training and practice, clear some space in your schedule, or stop coaching.

Know Your Role

The coach's role needs ongoing clarification in a healthy coaching system. As the framework for great coaching takes shape, a coaching culture can thrive. Take all the mystery out of coaching. Keep answering these questions by every means possible:

- What are we asking the coach to do?
- How is he supposed to help a church planter?
- What is your promise to the planter?
- What testimonials do you have from past planters about coaching?

For fruitful church planter coaching, the planter, the coach, and all church planting leaders must understand the role of the coach. Coaching, although vital, is not what's most important. The outcome—helping—is why we coach.

Healthy church plants are usually resourced by a crowd of helpers and encouragers, particularly in the first year. Denominational partners, along with local networks and sending churches, help church planters follow their calling to plant. However, as the "new" begins to wear away, the crowds often do as well. Church planter coaches provide the one-on-one support and long-term encouragement church planters need as the supporting crowds begin to shrink.

Great coaches challenge and encourage; they cheer and warn. But they never lose interest or go away. Great coaches abide with church planters. To maximize coaching fruitfulness, everybody involved must know their role.

"Coaching is an amazing way to create space and time to intentionally think, reflect, and process," according to Woody Wilson, church planter coach and coaching champion in Montreal. "Some of the biggest challenges are continually pushed to the back burner; with a coach there is intentionality, guidance, and accountability," Wilson added.

How Coaches Help Planters

The most painful part of struggling is the false belief that we shouldn't struggle. Our humanity is something we refuse to accept.

Elijah was well acquainted with what theologians call a "prophetic burden" of delivering a message he desperately wanted to be heard. Highlights from his ministry included raising a dead child to life and praying down an all-consuming fire from heaven. God received much glory through this man of faith.

As leaders, we are all tempted to believe that if we experienced such incredible victories in our ministries from God, we would never be discouraged again—ever. Yet with Elijah, this was not the case. Having faced incredible opposition in the past as well as perfectly good reasons to run and hide, he responded with bold faith. But something was different on the other side of Mount Carmel. The prophet with bold faith was despondent, sitting under a tree, scared for his life. What's wrong with this picture?

> And behold the word of the LORD came to him, and he said to him, "What are you doing here, Elijah?" He said, "I have been very jealous for the LORD, the God of hosts. For the people of Israel have forsaken your covenant, thrown down your altars, and killed your prophets with the sword, and I, even I only, am left, and they seek my life, to take it away." (1 Kings 19:9–10)

Jeff Christopherson gives a current interpretation to a timeless leadership challenge when he says, "The most difficult person you will ever have to lead is yourself."[3] No question Elijah was struggling with self-leadership in 1 Kings 19.

Mac Lake expanded this idea as well: "Leaders are visionaries. They think big, dream big and plan big. But sometimes the 'big' doesn't happen the way they envision. So they experience a 'big' disappointment."[4]

A coach helps church planters through diverse seasons of ministry. Often the challenges of serving God are as great during the winning seasons as they are in the losing ones. Planters and their families must not plant alone.

"Helping" needs more definition. What Elijah learned on the other side of Mount Carmel was as important as what he experienced on Mount Carmel when God defeated 450 prophets of Baal. How do planter coaches help planters?

Caring for their inner life is non-negotiable. How critical is your relationship with God and personal obedience in light of your kingdom assignment? Church planter Peter Scazzero issued this challenge:

> Beyond your strategy, programs, location, budget, launch team size, or facility, this one axiom always proves itself true: As goes the interior life of the church planter, so goes the church.[5]

Coaching Lesson 1: Coaches keep planters accountable for more than ministry performance and outcomes. The more robust the church planting system, the greater the danger of becoming a kingdom assembly line that is obsessed with output alone. Church planters are people, not cogs in our church-planting wheel.

Elite assessments and world-class training are critical. Never in my denomination's history have we been so close to offering such help to our planters. Yet the reason we invest in those vital processes is not to remove any possibility of failure. The reason is to partner with the people whom God entrusts to us and give them our best. Our passion is not merely to send, but to send well.

> Coaching Lesson 1: Coaches keep planters accountable for more than ministry performance and outcomes.

We are church planter coaches, and church planters are people. Most of them have families and friends who live under their roofs. Imperfect people with mental, physical, and emotional challenges (planter included) live there. Passionate disciples of all ages, as well as people who question the very existence of God, live there. No matter how things appear, seldom is everything as it ought to be with a planter's soul and the souls of those around him.

Our church planting systems are seldom designed for the broken people who populate them. Church planting is messy because the people involved are messy. Leaders are messy, like Elijah, who was burned out, severely depressed, borderline suicidal—all in spite of the fact that he deserved the status of "5-Star Prophet."

The goal is to deliver coaching systems that steward the lives and families whom God calls to plant churches. Coaching is the shepherding, compassionate, accountability arm of a healthy church planting system. Coaches must ask planters deeper questions to get beyond the surface in order to shepherd well.

Examples of Deeper Questions

- How are things between you and the Lord?
- What resting place with God can you rediscover over the next month?
- How are things with your wife and children?
- What can you do to encourage each of them over the next month?

Coaching Lesson 2: Coaches help planters focus on the dirty work. Coaches help planters eat frogs, or do the things that are not as fun. Eating frogs is messy and makes you change shirts often. The work with larger crowds is more enjoyable and is often the source of instant gratification.

God advised Elijah on his next steps in 1 Kings 19. The spirit of the advice seemed to be: "No more mountains for you; the real work on this side of the mountain is the development of more leaders."

The most important frogs in ministry are the ones you have to hold your nose and eat sushi style. The dirty work of making disciples and developing leaders takes more time and energy, but the long-term payoff is delicious! The future of the church and the expansion of the kingdom are in the development of multiplying leaders.

Examples of Leadership Development Coaching Questions

- What three leaders are you most hopeful about?
- What is your next step in developing each of them?
- Who on your Sunday morning team is ready for further development?
- When will you meet with these leaders to discuss next steps?

Coaching Lesson 3: Coaches help planters discover missing metrics and resources. Leaders are pathologically disappointed. That is the raw material God uses to make visionaries. Yet as with all leadership assets, this one has a dark side. Elijah's expectations on the other side of Mount Carmel were not being met, but they were unclear. Unclear expectations cannot be met! Leaders will, at times, obsess over the wrong metrics. Distancing themselves from other people as they sulk and feel ashamed of their shortcomings is a common response.

Examples of Isolation Coaching Questions

- How are you connected to other church planters?
- What steps can you take to be more connected?
- What wins are you overlooking?
- How can you celebrate these wins with others?

Helping planters shift their focus from isolation to community can be life- and ministry-saving. Satan loves to make leaders feel like they are "the only one."

Elijah was measuring success based on what he was doing and seeing while missing what God was doing. Obadiah hid one hundred prophets. Multitudes worshipped on Mount Carmel after the fire fell. God was in the fire and in the silence. And seven thousand others were guaranteed. Although you may feel alone, you are not. Elijah was believing a lie—that he was all alone. Coaches come alongside leaders and ask questions to help them see what is really happening.

Understand the Challenges Planters Face

Coaches must know their role and, as I like to say, "stay in their lane." Reviewing challenges is not to help you become a solutions expert or a person who fixes church planters. The best way to help the planter you coach is to let him be the expert. If he needs expert advice, let him find an expert or steer him toward one you might know.

You may be a former planter, a current planter, a missions pastor, or a sending church pastor. Maybe you are a business leader or professional coach. But understanding the challenges of planting will help you listen more attentively and ask relevant questions to help the planter stay in his role as expert.

Ed Stetzer[6] and Todd Wilson[7] did a study to discover the top challenges church planters faced. Although the research was not scientific, it was substantive. A large number of veteran planters, from Rick Warren to John Worcester, were consulted, and online surveys were conducted from current planters through Exponential.

The list of discoveries was reduced to the "Top 7 Challenges Facing Church Planters." This paper is invaluable for every church planter coach.[8]

Below I added sample questions to help a planter process the most common challenges with his coach. As with all lists of questions, view these as starter questions to help the planter discover places to go deeper.

Note that coaching through this list of challenges would easily populate an entire year of coaching. Particularly when you see the words *adjustment, upgrade,* and *attention*—these never end. Yet a coach can help a planter maintain focus and keep working in the right places.

Don't limit yourself to these questions. Let the planter's answers inspire deeper questions. If not, you will come across as an interrogating coach. You don't want to be that kind of coach.

Top 7 Challenges Facing Church Planters

1. Leadership development and reproducing culture

   - What is your plan to develop leaders?
   - What is going well?
   - What part of your leadership development plan needs upgrading or adjusting?

2. Financial self-sufficiency and viability

   - How are you developing generous disciples?
   - What is your next step?
   - How do you need to engage your current donors?

3. Team development and volunteer mobilization

   - What's working in your current volunteer mobilization approach?
   - What's working in your overall team development?
   - What needs more of your attention now?

4. Systems, processes, and cultures

   - What systems need upgrading to sustain your current growth?
   - What disciples are you personally developing?
   - What is your next step to develop them?

5. Vision casting and avoiding mission drift

   - What is your biggest distraction?
   - What is your church's biggest distraction?
   - What steps can you take to refocus?

6. Evangelism and discipleship

- How can you serve your community more effectively?
- How is your church reaching lost people?
- How can you strengthen what is already working?

7. Spiritual, physical, and mental health of planter and family

- How can I become a better coach for you?
- What can you do over the next thirty days to serve your wife?
- What can you change to provide more balance in your life?[9]

Church planters and their families begin with bold faith and high expectations. The thread of expectations is evident through every challenge. Clint Clifton's "Expectations Worksheet" is found in Appendix F along with key questions to help planters process their expectations. Help the planter you coach work through this tool every six months his first two years. Ask tough questions— these coaching conversations can be game changers.

With Fear and Trembling

Scott Thomas of Gospel Coach, the former president of Acts 29, reviewed a series of tragedies in the lives of church planters in his network. He concluded, "Shepherding and coaching can be one ministry, not two." As he struggled over the realties church planters face, he resolved:

> We want every pastor and church leader to be a qualified, Gospel-empowered, healthy, disciple-making follower of Jesus leading others to the Chief Shepherd. Coaching ministry leaders is a key aspect to their ongoing effectiveness as shepherds of the Lord's flock.[10]

Church planters need strong coaches who love Jesus, His mission, and them as well. Don't take your church planter coaching lightly. Do whatever it takes to communicate this message to the next church planter you coach:

I can help you!

Be Coached . . .

1. What adjustments can you make for your coaching to become more helpful?

2. Which of the "Top 7 Challenges Planters Face" surprised you the most?

3. What challenge was left off the list?

4. What church planter can you encourage in the next thirty days?

My Coach Helps . . .

My coach helps me process the challenges of life and leadership in ministry. My coaching relationships have provided the additional perspective needed to better understand where I needed to grow and how to lead the church more effectively. No matter how big of a dreamer and thinker you are, your perspective is never big enough. Surrounding yourself with coaches that can inspire and challenge you cultivates wisdom. Wisdom is an essential quality of leadership. Wisdom is never gained in a vacuum.

Rick Ackerman
5280 Church
Denver, Colorado
www.5280church.com

 **CHAPTER 3**

Discover Church Planter Coaches

John and his wife, Connie, were our small group leaders. Yvette (my wife) and I experienced an incredible season of growth under their leadership. We deeply valued the biblical community we enjoyed over those four years.

Life had taken a dramatic change for me. My new position as Church Planter Coaching Director for the North American Mission Board was daunting. My responsibilities expanded dramatically from delivering coaching and training small groups of coaches to creating systems that could operate without me in cities across North America.

John was an engineer who designed automated systems to clean the inside of oil tankers all around the world. I loved spending time with John, and I needed a systems expert with an outside perspective. So it made sense to ask him for some practical advice.

We met at a local sandwich shop for lunch that summer. "Explain to me how a system works," I asked. With pen and a napkin in hand, John drew a simple illustration that explained how his tanker cleaning system worked.

I don't remember many details, but I will never forget the "moment" of the conversation with my friend. John stopped in the middle of drawing, looked over the top of his glasses at me, and smiled. "Pipe is easy to work with because you can predict and control the variables," John said. "But remember, people are not pipe."

Three Variables in Coaching Systems

God did not hardwire me to be a systems engineer. But my conversation with John left a lasting impression. The challenge we faced became clearer that day. My first step was to identify the variables. Then, I needed to discover what our church planter coaching system could and could not influence.

Variable 1: The Holy Spirit

Heather Bond, a church-planting wife in Sidney, British Columbia, has seen the value of coaching firsthand for her husband, Matthew. Heather described the influence of a coach:

> Coaching is like noise-canceling headphones; it takes all those voices, internal and external, in Matthew's life and helps him discern which one is the Holy Spirit's.[1]

Jesus promised, "But the Helper, the Holy Spirit, whom the Father will send in my name, he will teach you all things and bring to your remembrance all that I have said to you" (John 14:26). A planter may plan what to do next, but how can he know what God wants? His coach may decide what question to ask, but does he sense the leadership of the Holy Spirit in his coaching? Coaching without the awareness and work of the Holy Spirit will produce activity without fruit.

Tony Stoltzfus said, "Coaching is about having faith in the heart-changing power of the Holy Spirit."[2] None of us would claim to understand the mysterious work of the Holy Spirit. As with the wind, we do not move the Holy Spirit; the Holy Spirit moves us.

One desired outcome in our one-day coach orientation is for each coach to have someone listen to them, put a hand on their shoulder, and pray for them. Numerous times this happens over the course of the day. Leaders usually do all the listening and praying for others. This day is their day to receive as well.

At the end of each day, we ask coaches to share personal highlights with the group. One Thursday afternoon in Atlanta, a coach attempted to give his highlight but was overcome with emotion. When he collected himself, he explained, "Most events I attend I create. I open the building, set up the room, provide the food, and do the training." He apologized for what he was about to say because it sounded so selfish. "But today was all about me," he confessed.

My passion for coaching leaders intensified more that day in Atlanta. Who shepherds the shepherds? Who listens to the one who is always there to offer a listening ear? Who cares for the caregiver? No question: on that day, a host of coaches had listened, cared, and prayed for this weary leader. And God through His Holy Spirit had given rest to his soul.

Each time I hear peer coaches coach each other, I wonder how many leaders are missing the benefits of coaching. What if every church planter in your city had this kind of relationship? What difference would it make? Coaches led by the Holy Spirit provide soul care for weary church planters.

> Coaches led by the Holy Spirit provide soul care for weary church planters.

Coaching cultures and systems can create a dependence on the skills of a coach. We want to create systems that depend not on the skills of the coach, but on the heart of the coach, and more important, on the work of the Holy Spirit through a life-giving relationship.

Variable 2: The Church Planter

Church planters are always looking for advice. But a shepherding, asking coach is unfamiliar. Planters are reluctant to add to a daunting list of daily meetings, tasks, and commitments. But once they experience the value of great coaching, they will want more.

For example, Buff McNickle moved from Florida to Atlantic City, New Jersey, to plant Great Falls Church in 2013. Buff described an immediate return on his time invested in being coached: "I quickly realized this wasn't another task or burden, but truly a blessing if done well and consistently for a season."

Buff further commented on the value he received from a church planter coach:

> My coach helped me truly know what it means to "walk in step with the Spirit." Our coaching sessions helped me to think, track, and take the necessary steps to help me live out the mission of God in my church plant and everyday life. His ability to draw out my thoughts and move me forward to action has helped tremendously.

Buff had a great coach who influenced his coachability. We are quick to blame the planter for his lack of interest in coaching. But coaches may bear part of the responsibility.

Church planters may have perfectly good reasons for resisting your best intentions to coach them. The following ten factors will lower the planter's coachability. A church planter may:

1. Already have a coach.
2. Think he already has a coach.
3. Misunderstand the role of a coach.
4. Have had a bad coach in the past.
5. Know someone who had a bad coach.
6. Feel no connection with his assigned coach.
7. Question the credibility of his coach.
8. Struggle to manage time and tasks.
9. Mistrust your motives.
10. Have more perfectly good reasons not listed.

Evaluating current coaching relationships and teaching your coaches to do the same will help build trust and raise interest in being coached. Coaches should ask questions like:

How can I become a better coach for you?

What can I change to make this time more productive for you?

What tasks do you need to complete between now and when we talk again?

As you learn more about obstacles to coachability in your area, you will discover ones you can influence. My friend John was right; people are not pipe. But you can address these variables with your team of coaches and planters.

Work on Your Coachability

Planters must own the responsibility for their coachability as well. With a few adjustments, planters can get more from their next coach. Coaches, if you are not coachable, you are probably not a good coach. Every coach needs a coach.

> Every coach needs a coach.

Variable 3: The Coach

The coach in your system is the one variable that you can influence the most. Your system needs discovery, development, and deployment processes. Here are three questions for you to answer to help get your system:

- Discovery: Who makes a great church planter coach candidate?
- Deployment: How do I prepare coaches to coach?
- Development: How do I set coaches up for success?

Discovery: Who Makes a Great Coaching Candidate?

My father opened an Italian Restaurant in East Tennessee in 1963. He claimed to serve the first lasagna in history for the region. He confessed in his later years that he guessed at the claim, but over fifty years later it has yet to be challenged.

I affectionately called him the "accidental entrepreneur." Untrained and uneducated in business, he seemed to know the right things to do. His simple success plan was: serve great lasagna, name the business after yourself, love people every place you go, and go lots of places. But he believed in what he sold. And he understood that people were not required to buy. They had options.

If you are a coach, you must believe in what you sell—the "why" behind what you do. If you are developing coaches, you must sell them to your planters. The value of the relationship must far outweigh the cost. "Because coaching is a requirement" doesn't work well with church planters. Planters may agree on those terms, but the influence of coaching will be limited.

Look for coaches who will be easy to sell. Soon in the process you will be having a conversation with a planter about his coach or his options for coaches. How difficult will it be for you to convince him of the value of the coaching process and the creditability of the coach? This perspective creates a filter for those whom you invite to coach planters. Will planters want to be coached by your coaches?

In Appendix I, you will find a more detailed "Credibility and Capacity Checklist" to help you filter potential coach candidates. The checklist provides a template for you to create your own. You can train to enhance skills, but church planter coaches must bring certain qualities with them to become great coaches.

Three basic traits to look for in new church planter coaches are:

- Fruit of the good work of Jesus
- Full engagement in God's mission
- A heart to develop leaders

Fruit of the Good Work of Jesus

Fruit of the good work of Jesus is what you see in a growing disciple. Paul described the transformational journey: "And I am sure of this, that he who began a good work in you will bring it to completion at the day of Jesus Christ" (Phil. 1:6).

Coach, take a moment to consider these questions:

- Who am I becoming?
- What has God changed in me over the past year?

- What is God attempting to change in me now?
- What am I learning?
- How is my approach to life and ministry changing?
- Who is my coach, and how often do we connect?
- What friends and mentors speak boldly into my life?

The above questions are critical for great coaches. We should review them often and make the necessary adjustments to keep moving forward in our relationship with Christ. Those we invite to become coaches should demonstrate a desire to grow and the corresponding humility that reflects the good work of Jesus.

Full Engagement in God's Mission

Here are four entry-level questions to consider for a church planter coach candidate:

1. How is he personally involved in God's mission?
2. How is he leading others to be involved in God's mission?
3. What evidence do you see that he loves church planters?
4. What level of involvement and support does he give church planting?

The coach provides an asking and shepherding voice among the voices that speak into the life of a planter and his family. In our system, a coach does not necessarily need to be a planter. But the four entry-level questions establish important coach criteria.

A Heart to Develop Leaders

Becoming a mature coach who develops leaders well is a lifetime process. But the best coaches have shown evidence of advancement through the following levels:

Level I: The Helicopter Coach (All about the project)—*I want to help your plant.* This level is about the planter's immaturity and lack of skills to lead his new church. The first level of development obsesses on the project (plant) at the expense of the planter.

Working on the project is part of the coaching relationship, but not all of the relationship.

Level II: The Guru Coach (All about me)—*I want to help you be like me.* This level is all about my skills, strengths, and insights as a coach. The second level of development obsesses on the coach at the expense of the planter. Learning from the coach is part of the relationship, but not all of the relationship.

Level III: The Shepherd Coach (All about Jesus)—*I want to help you be better than I am.* This level is about all King Jesus has planned for the planter. The third level focuses on the planter's development in the present and the future. Jesus made an amazing promise to the disciples:

> "Truly, truly, I say to you, whoever believes in me will also do the works that I do; and greater works than these will he do, because I am going to the Father." (John 14:12)

Jesus revealed His agenda: *You will do greater works than I do, and that is all a part of My plan.* Emotionally healthy coaches can learn much from Jesus' earthly ministry. Am I spiritually mature enough to watch the people I coach do greater works than I do?

Level III coaches grasp the importance of all King Jesus has planned for the planter. Everything is urgent in the early days of a church planter's journey. But patience and persistence are part of the coach's role. Find coaches who have a history of developing leaders. And help your current coaches understand and advance through the coaching levels.

The Biggest Question

Coaching qualifications are local decisions. A one-size-fits-all answer to the question is impossible. You know your planters, and you know your potential coaches. What do you want your coach to do for the planter he coaches? The answer to this question is critical to creating a list of qualifications.

The single greatest influence on your coaching culture or brand will be your coaches. Be leery of casting too large a net for coaches with the intention of providing every planter a coach. Build a coaching system that lasts by beginning with the best coaches for your planters.

Deployment: How Do I Prepare Coaches to Coach?

New coach orientation is the first step in launching a church planter coaching system. Regardless of the level of coaching experience or training history of the coaches, you need a day together getting everybody on the same page. The following questions are important to answer:

- What is meant by the term *coach?*
- Who else is on the coaching team?
- How does a coaching relationship look?
- How long does a coaching relationship last?
- How can I tell that my coaching is working?
- How can I grow as a coach?
- Who can help me?
- Who else around me should be coaching?

Coaching relationships should complement church planting conversations already happening in assessments, training, and networks. Church planters live in a busy world. Coaching is an intersection where many roads meet, not another road with new obligations.

Orientation vs. Training

Bob Logan is the first person I heard describe the difference between orientation and training. Although it may seem insignificant at first, it provides a valuable perspective. Bob described the difference this way:

Many people misname orientation. They call it training. But in fact, we can't train in a classroom; we can only give people enough to get them started. Then, as they're out doing the work, when they start running into roadblocks and asking questions, then is the time to deliver just-in-time training.[3]

Think of the orientation meetings for incoming first-year students at your local college. Freshmen are preparing for a long, challenging four-year journey. Everything a college freshman needs to know cannot possibly be covered in a few days. The most important need for college freshmen is to understand the process and start strong.

Orientation for coaches starts the process. Participants have already agreed to coach planters. Our one-day orientation experience covers five principles and five practices of church planter coaching. We want our coaches to understand the process and start strong. More information will be needed in the future but is not yet relevant.

Peer coaching relationships are established at orientation. Peer coaches coach each other during orientation and continue with four conversations afterward. A coach mentor joins the fourth conversation to give feedback on the progress of each coach.

After peer coaching, local planting leaders assign coaches to planters. Every coach will not be a match to every church planter. Care is given to make good matchups. Coaching takes place eight months a year with a total of sixteen conversations. We recommend two coaching conversations a month over four months. But as always, our way is only a template for you to create your way.

Developing a team of coaches (we call them coaching pods) is the next step. Pods exist for the communication, encouragement, and growth of coaches. Pods also keep an active team prepared to be assigned or reassigned to planters. You can find a visual overview of our coach deployment process in Appendix C: "Multiply Coaches for the Mission."

Development: How Do I Set Coaches Up for Success?

Help your coaches start strong. Developing coaches who exhibit great coaching behaviors is an ongoing process, but a high level of intentionality is vital in the early stages. What do new coaches need to know to start strong? The answer to this question helps you build out your coaching system. Coaching starts strong when:

1. *Coaches understand their role in the lives of planters.* No matter how you define the role, you help set the agenda for the relationship. Then you train, resource, and evaluate your coaches accordingly.

2. *Coaches are aware of how the planters are trained.* We create coaching guides that familiarize coaches with training content. We don't ask our coaches to become church planting tutors. But our coaches ask questions that help planters review and implement what they have already learned.

3. *Coaches are familiar with the other voices: consulting, mentoring, training, and supervision.* A church planting brotherhood evolves through a community of leaders committed to sending well. If a potential coach is relationally disconnected with other church planting voices, he is not a strong coaching candidate. Your influence on the coach will be limited, too, which creates more potential problems.

4. *Coaches are not asked to wear multiple hats.* As practical as "multiple hats" sounds, it takes away from great coaching. Church planters, Sending Church pastors, friends, and church planting leaders already wear multiple hats. Coaches coach best when they wear their coaching hat.

5. *The planter clearly understands the role of the coach.* A coaching agreement clarifies the coach's purpose. Use a written agreement to help planters understand the coaching process. An example of a coaching agreement is in Appendix G.

Coaches, coaching leaders, and coach developers can influence every variable that makes a system deliver great coaching to every church planter. Look closely at the three variables and take responsibility: the Holy Spirit, the Church Planter, and the Coach. Never allow this irresponsible, dangerous attitude to be a part of your culture:

That's out of our control.

People are not pipe, but they can be influenced through consistent and courageous leadership. The right question to ask about your system is:

What can we do about this challenge?

Be Coached . . .

1. What could you do to increase coachability in coaches?

2. What could you do to increase coachability in planters?

3. What do you want your coaches or your coaching to do for planters?

4. What is your next step?

My Coach Helps . . .

A few years into a new church plant, I realized that despite my best efforts, I wasn't making the progress I wanted in my life and ministry. My coach came alongside me and helped me find focus, gain tools in time management, and take steps in my marriage and family. Coaching moved me from being a struggling youth pastor overseeing a few people to a confident executive pastor overseeing hundreds of people and multiple ministries.

Dustyn Burwell
Greater European Mission Church Planter
Dublin, Ireland
www.gemadventure.com/missionaries/burwell

 **CHAPTER 4**

Clarify Coaching Principles

Peter Scazzero and his wife Geri planted New Life Church in Queens, New York, in 1987. Although the work has prospered over the years, there have been incredibly dark days as well.[1]

Scazzero has openly chronicled the struggles in his marriage as well as his church in his books, including *Emotionally Healthy Spirituality* and *The Emotionally Healthy Church Planter*. We need emotionally healthy coaches and planters—every planter and coach should read both.

Scazzero described the challenges church planters face:

> The challenges and stresses of church planting introduce us to ourselves. It makes us face the harshest realities in our lives, the monsters within, our shadows, and our self-will that resists God's will.[2]

Coaching helps leaders gain focus, solve problems, and turn truth into action. But on a deeper level, the challenges of ministry are greater than day-to-day operations. Leaders are pathologically disappointed and perpetually overwhelmed. Like vending machines, they provide for the hungry masses daily.

Challenges are not limited to church-related demands. Personal finances, marriage, and children require attention, yet planters seldom have the time or emotional capacity to give. Spiritual, physical, and emotional health usually fall to the bottom of the list.

The results can be disastrous. The primary reason a planter needs a coach is that he needs help.

Five Coaching Principles

Coaching principles are an important part of the platform of a coaching system. Random philosophies of coaching generate random results. Building a system takes time and repetition. But church planters, their families, and their churches reap the benefits.

> The primary
> reason a
> planter needs
> a coach is that
> he needs help.

Most church planting leaders need more planter coaches than they can produce. Building a system that multiplies great coaching takes time. Most of our cities take two to three years before we see significant progress. But if leaders choose to take shortcuts, then nothing substantive will ever be produced.

One of our outcomes for the first part of our one-day coach orientation is this: when I say "coach" and you say "coach," we are talking about the same thing. The details about how a coaching conversation should look, how often one should happen, and the desired outcomes are vital to the church planter's benefit.

You may have different ideas about what principles will shape your coaching and the coaches you develop. Here is what is important:

- Choose specific principles.
- Build training and coaching culture on those principles.
- Stay consistent.

Principles provide a quality control platform to measure results. Also, principles inform how you will resource your active coaches. If you want great coaches, everyone must know what you want them to be great at doing. This chapter provides a brief summary of our five principles.

Principle 1: Every leader needs a coach.

Earlier in my ministry, I might have disagreed with the statement *every leader needs a coach*, particularly when describing a coach who is the asking and listening kind. But when I moved from an old office building in urban Cincinnati to a new office in South Carolina complete with full-time assistants, a big budget, and the best technology, things dramatically changed.

Even in the midst of extraordinary resources, I felt overmatched and afraid. I preferred my former environment that was built on relationships and responding to needs. I didn't know how to build a church planting system from the ground up. I needed expert advice, so I pursued one of the most influential church planting leaders in North America: Bob Logan.

Months into my new role, my team started to grow, as did my relationship with Bob. My team members had skills and experiences I didn't, yet I was their leader. In one memorable coaching conversation, I asked, "How can I help them, Bob? They're ahead of me." In a rare moment of impatience and emotion, Coach Bob responded, "Coaching! It's coaching—you need to coach them!"

Other coaches have influenced me since my first conversations with Bob:

- Bill helped me discover a healthier lifestyle.
- Glenn helped me develop my inner entrepreneur.
- Steve, Tony, and Laura helped me develop my skills as a coach.
- Geoff challenged me as a disciple of Jesus, husband, dad, and granddad.

I learned the importance of focus, accountability, and action. Most of all, my approach to life was transformed, and my trajectory in ministry changed. The table below shows the value coaching brings to any leader:

Leader's Need	Coaching Benefit	Helpful Questions
Processing	Clarity	"Where do you need to go next?" "What's important now?"
Planning	Action	"How do you need to get there?" "When do you need to start?"
Assessing	Discovery	"What do you need?" "Who can help you?"
Debriefing	Accountability	"How is your plan working?" "What adjustments are needed?"

Leading leaders is different from leading followers. Followers are crucial to the health and effectiveness of the body of Christ; they are truly gifts from God. They gladly serve, work hard, and wait for instructions on what to do next. Leaders are different.

An emerging leader is not waiting for orders from the top of the organizational chart. Church planters have an apostolic impulse, a clear vision, and entrepreneurial leanings. For them to grow, they need to be engaged—like Jesus engaged His team.

Leaders learn through dialogue. They process out loud. Two key practices of a great coach are listening and asking. These two disciplines, central to coaching, can help form a foundation of healthy leadership development.

No matter the specifics of any assignment, leaders tend to focus on acquiring better skills, strategies, and learning best practices. But unfortunately, the resulting to-do list creates slaves to the moment, neglecting deeper and more important issues. We've all been there.

> Great coaching works on the worker, not just the work.

Great coaching exposes ways the planter needs to grow. Great coaching works on the worker, not just the work. Every church planter needs a to-do list, but he also needs a to-be list. The to-do list is for the urgent, but the to-be list is for a lifetime. Every church planter needs a coach.

Principle 2: Coaching is simple.

Coaching is simple—but don't confuse simple with easy. Great church planter coaching requires training, practice, and skill. To help good coaches become great coaches, we must define what we want them to be great at doing.

Most people connect the word *coach* to sports. Effective athletic coaches fill multiple roles in the lives of their players. Teacher, mentor, parent, trainer, and supervisor are typical coaching responsibilities. Their ultimate mission is to bring out the best in players to help the team win.

The multiple roles of an athletic coach, carried into planter coaching, can create redundancy. Think back through the list of responsibilities. How many of those roles are filled? Too many people doing the same thing disregards what is needed most or what may already be happening. Planter fatigue and confusion are unintended results.

Steve Addison, in his valuable tool titled "The Start-Up Guide to Coaching Leaders," gives a simple definition of coaching:

> The relational process of co-operating with the Holy Spirit that unlocks a person's God-given potential so that they become more like Christ and make their unique contribution to the Kingdom.[3]

Coaching is a tool in your leadership development toolbox. Coaching is not better than counseling, advising, teaching, or mentoring—but it is different. Mentoring, teaching, advising, and counseling are devalued without a clear definition of coaching. The ultimate loser in such a scenario is the church planter. *How is coaching different?*

Coaching is different from counseling. A counselor helps solve a personal crisis. Counselors function much like emergency room doctors, addressing a current pain point. ER doctors start with pain and hope to provide both temporary relief and long-term healing.

The key word for counselors is *relief*. Part of the counseling process involves reaching into the past to help people understand how they got to their current pain point (marriage, parenting, financial, career, etc.) and moving to the present.

As emergency room doctors, counselors are instruments of help and healing. They are committed "to cure sometimes, to relieve often, to comfort always." Discerning coaches know when the planter they coach needs a counselor, and they make referrals without hesitation. But coaches are different from counselors.

Coaching is different from advising. An advisor or consultant assesses needs and provides solutions. An advisor has a role similar to that of an auto mechanic, who focuses on what is broken or needs to be maintained. He advises your need for an oil change or tire rotation to keep your car in optimal running condition. He also tells you when you need a brake job or a new water pump and will fix these things for you if you would like.

The key word for advisors is *solutions*. Advisors process their life experiences, watch other people, do research, and put all those facets together to create formulas for success. Does it work? Absolutely—at times, in places. Is advising based on biblical principles? Yes: "Without counsel plans fail, but with many advisers they succeed" (Prov. 15:22). Advising can be helpful when based on biblical wisdom. But coaches are different from advisors.

Coaching is different from teaching. A teacher explains helpful and sometimes life-changing information, much like a librarian. Teaching is valuable; Jesus Himself was a master teacher.

The key word for teachers is *information*. I have enjoyed the benefit of strong Bible teachers for most of my life. And the incredible influence of teachers is not limited to Bible teachers who help me grow in Christ. I have been taught to do everything—from tying my shoe to cooking breakfast.

My life would be dramatically different without the influence of great teachers. And teaching is biblical: "Him we proclaim, warning everyone and teaching everyone with all wisdom, that we may present everyone mature in Christ" (Col. 1:28). But coaches are different from teachers.

Coaching is different from mentoring. A mentor imparts wisdom from his or her reservoir of personal experiences, successes, and failures. Like a personal trainer, a mentor helps you become what he or she has become. The lists below show us the differences:

Drawing Out (Coach)	Pouring In (Mentor)
Develops	Reproduces
Asks How	Tells How
Supports	Imparts Wisdom
Uber Driver	Personal Trainer
Barnabas	Paul

The key word for mentors is *imitation*. The Bible describes mentoring through Paul's example. He was Timothy's mentor. Paul identified the principle of mentoring when he told Corinthian believers to: "be imitators of me, as I am of Christ" (1 Cor. 11:1). Leaders need both coaches and mentors. Although they may overlap, mentoring and coaching are most effective when received in different relationships. But coaches are different from mentors.

Coaching is different. A coach helps a leader move forward in pursuit of their relationship with God and their unique kingdom assignment. A coach is like a taxi driver. Drivers share their vehicle to help you get to places you need to be. The passenger sets the destination in a highly relational process. The driver serves the passenger by getting them to the next place in a safe and timely manner.

The key word for coaches is *implementation*. A great coach helps leaders turn truth into action. The role of a coach is unique— it's not to be another voice talking to the planter, as important as some of those voices are. A coach comes alongside a church planter to draw out what is already being poured in.

How Coaching Is Different

Role	Counselor	Advisor	Teacher	Mentor	Coach
Function	ER Doctor	Auto Mechanic	Librarian	Personal Trainer	Taxi Driver
Key Word	Relief	Solutions	Information	Imitation	Service
Scripture	Proverbs 13:20	Proverbs 15:22	Colossians 1:28	1 Corinthians 11:1	Proverbs 20:5

A coach's voice is the asking voice, and the coach's most basic tools are listening well and asking questions. A church planter coach fulfills his role on the team by providing a safe place for an often-overwhelmed church planter.

The writer in Proverbs illustrates this coaching principle: "The purpose in a man's heart is like deep water, but a man of understanding will draw it out" (Prov. 20:5).

Counselors, advisors, teachers, and mentors provide important relationships to help us move forward in living out God's unique kingdom assignment. But don't leave out the coach; every leader needs one.

Coaching is simple—anyone can do it by learning to listen and ask. But coaching is not easy; great church planter coaching requires training, practice, and skill.

Principle 3: Coaches advance God's mission.

When Jesus said, "'Therefore pray earnestly to the Lord of the harvest to send out laborers into his harvest'" (Matt. 9:38), He was inviting us to be part of the sending as well as the harvesting.

Coaching is a way to expand your personal sending capacity through intentional relationships with church planters. As we study today's church planting landscape, we realize that sending more is not the only answer—we must also send *well*. We believe achieving this overarching goal begins here:

Intentional relationships + scheduled conversations

Those intentional relationships and scheduled conversations don't just happen on their own. A clear plan and purpose are vital to the success of church planter coaching. Below are characteristics of effective church planter coaching relationships:

- **One-on-one instead of in groups.** Most planters are already in active relational networks and group coaching. Another need is one-on-one interaction with a safe person—someone who can objectively help them process what God is doing.
- **Sequential rather than random.** We all know what happens with random relationships: no matter their value, they eventually die due to time demands. Good coaching is sequential—ideally every other week in four-month bursts.
- **Integrated, not competing.** Coaching complements what God is already doing in planters' lives. Coaching also leverages what is being said during assessments, trainings, and networking—challenging the planter to turn truth into action.
- **Mission coaching, not life coaching.** Church planter coaching utilizes coaching guides that help the planter focus on both personal growth and planting results. At times the coach will push toward topics that serve the best interest of God's mission versus letting the planter set the agenda.
- **By phone rather than through face-to-face interactions.** The goal is to be consistent and focused. Consistency is more important than proximity. Phone or video conference

conversations are more time efficient and easier to manage for many than face-to-face interactions.

Principle 4: Coaches target the heart.

As God began to break new ground in my life, my confidence in His ability to work in and through people around me soared. My confidence was in the unique, one-on-one environment the coaching relationship created. A coaching relationship gave God space to work in people—myself included.

Our tendency as leaders is to go fast and get quick results. So we focus on symptoms versus heart issues. Symptoms are urgent; we need relief. We view symptoms as mere obstacles in the way of progress. We prefer bandages over surgery—yet this is seldom the right choice.

For transformation to happen in the lives of church planters, coaches should target the heart. Here are some questions that can help begin deeper heart conversations:

- What does God want?
- What is God saying?
- What is really happening here?
- What is really important?
- What is God attempting to change in you now?

These questions are a great starting point for diving deep into the heart of the person you coach. But there's more—we all have desires deep inside us, things we know we must target if our lives are to be successful.

No matter how much we succeed in other pursuits, nothing will ever replace five critical desires (heart hungers) God has given us. In the coaching conversations I have experienced over the years, these five concerns eventually came to the top of the list:

Peter Scazzero wrote:

Lord, I ask that you would not simply heal the symptoms of what is not right in my life, but that you would surgically remove all that is in me that does not belong to you.[4]

Scazzero's prayer is powerful and courageous. Coaches need to pray this prayer first to experience the same transformation we hope for in those we coach.

Principle 5: Coaches embrace biblical values.

Coaches believe God can transform the life and ministry of the planters they coach. A church planter benefits from having a coach who embraces biblical values and incorporates them into his coaching.

As leaders, we usually default to offering great answers to the people we lead to help them grow. But when we take our default too far, we miss one of the best answers we could ever give: a great question.

The Bible is full of questions. The first question God ever asked is in Genesis 3. God asked Adam a question. God did not need an answer, but Adam needed a question:

> And they heard the sound of the LORD God walking in the garden in the cool of the day, and the man and his wife hid themselves from the presence of the LORD God among the trees of the garden. But the LORD God called to the man and said to him, "Where are you?" (Gen. 3:8–9)

The God of the universe—the One who is all-knowing, all-present, all-powerful—chose to ask instead of tell. God didn't shout out with a voice of thunder, "I see you over there in those bushes, Adam, and I see Eve, too." Why not?

God chose a different tool—for Adam's benefit. God knew what He had planned. Adam's world was falling apart because of his choice to turn away from God instead of toward Him. God asked a simple question to draw Adam out of hiding: Where are you?

Fast forward to the New Testament—Jesus constantly asked His disciples questions:

> Now when Jesus came into the district of Caesarea Philippi, he asked his disciples, "Who do people say that the Son of Man is?" And they said, "Some say John the Baptist, others say Elijah, and others Jeremiah or one of the prophets." He said to them, "But who do you say that I am?" Simon Peter replied, "You are the Christ, the Son of the living God." (Matt. 16:13–16)

Both passages illustrate one simple point: asking is an effective way to influence someone toward God's purposes and ways. But is the fact that God the Father, Jesus, and many others in the Bible asked questions enough to cause us to pursue coaching? Of course not. Everyone who speaks asks questions. We must get to the heart of the matter—why do we ask questions as coaches? We ask because:

1. God is at work in the life of each person we coach.
2. The people we coach have the ability to hear God.
3. The people we coach need to learn how to hear God.
4. We do not know all the answers.
5. Each person we coach has a unique assignment from God.
6. An unhealthy dependence on an advice-giver does not produce a leader, only a follower.

Coaching isn't magic or a more excellent way. God can, however, use coaches for His purpose if they focus on coaching well. Coaches embrace biblical values: they believe the Holy Spirit can transform church planters.

Five principles for church planter coaching:

1. Every leader needs a coach.
2. Coaching is simple.
3. Coaches advance God's mission.
4. Coaches target the heart.
5. Coaches embrace biblical values.

Be Coached . . .

1. What principle is most important to you?

2. What principle would you add?

3. What principle is most relevant to your personal coaching now?

4. What step will you take to upgrade your coaching as a result?

My Coach Helps . . .

My coach helps me work through all areas of my life. I simply desire to lead better—in my marriage, my parenting, my spiritual life, my staff, my leaders, and my church. People that pursue coaching will become better leaders of leaders. My spiritual, mental, and physical health are better off for pursuing coaching.

Keith Baldridge
The Living Stone Church
Broomfield, CO
www.thelivingstone.church

 **PART 2**

Develop Great Coaching

"Great coaches come alongside leaders so leaders can be transformed into the image of Christ and join Him on His redemptive mission."[1]

The following list of coaching qualities represents a unique combination of heart and skill. As you read the next ten chapters, celebrate how God has made you. Then make plans to become a great coach. No one is a "10" in every coaching quality. And you currently possess certain qualities that will help you coach. In fact, you are probably using these qualities more than you know.

Other qualities will develop through practice. Evidence of the ten qualities in people around you will also help you discover future coaches, coach mentors, and coaching champions.

What Are the Qualities of a Great Coach?

Serving

Serving and giving are core coaching practices. Coaches enjoy helping others win. Jesus' mission was to serve and give: "'For even the Son of Man came not to be served but to serve, and to give his life as a ransom for many'" (Mark 10:45).

Believing

What drives a great coach is the core belief in God's ability to change people. Paul's encouraging words are the lens through which coaches see the planters they coach: "And I am sure of this, that he who began a good work in you will bring it to completion at the day of Jesus Christ" (Phil. 1:6).

Listening

People are drawn to listeners, not talkers. People talk to us twenty-four hours a day—if not in person, then via podcasts, social media, email, etc. But a great coach is a great listener. Great listeners ask insightful questions because they are genuinely curious about another person's story. They also listen to what God is doing in the heart of the storyteller.

Cheering

Barnabas was nicknamed the "son of encouragement." He took John Mark on a mission trip even when Paul thought it was a bad decision. Great coaches come alongside church planters and help them celebrate wins. They help church planters get out of demoralizing ruts in life and ministry to move forward again.

Praying

Bob Logan said, "At its core, coaching is a spiritual process."[2] Great coaches invite God into the process of the coaching relationship, praying with and for the person they coach. Great coaches also understand that the only long-term wins in life and ministry come from God's working in the heart.

Pressing

"Therefore, preparing your minds for action, and being sober-minded, set your hope fully on the grace that will be brought to you at the revelation of Jesus Christ" (1 Pet. 1:13). Most of us lose focus under pressure. Whether the pressure is from family struggles, financial issues, or a fear of failing, a coach can help a leader gain clarity and take action. A coach will not only ask the right questions but will also keep the planter he coaches accountable for taking action.

Supporting

Everything doesn't work everywhere for everybody. This principle certainly applies to life and ministry. Every church planter has a unique kingdom assignment. Variables abound: the location of a new church, the timing of a planting project, and the attributes of the planter (his background, gifts, and experience) are only a few. What works in Vancouver may not work in the Bronx or Miami. The coach must provide support for the church planter regardless of these variables, in whatever context the planter is serving.

Relating

Coaching is a relationship, and relationships take time. Coaching involves intentional, one-on-one conversations that require patience, listening, and asking questions. Coaching is more of a process than a discussion about a particular topic. A great coach is comfortable with an ongoing, relational journey toward God's purposes.

Growing

Tony Stoltzfus wrote, "Great coaching springs out of fully embracing the work of God in your own life."[3] Great coaches are growing disciples and lifetime learners. Great coaching is a matter of the heart, but coaches want to improve their skills as well. Measuring the effectiveness of their coaching and asking for feedback from the planters they coach are routine practices.

Planting

The framework for church planter coaching includes the church planter in pursuit of his unique kingdom assignment.

Great coaches are passionate about how that assignment fits into the bigger picture of God's glory and the gospel. Thus, they care deeply about the outcome. A coach embraces his role as a helper who walks beside the planter. He understands he is not the only voice in the planter's life.

Great coaches are made, not born. Part 2 of *Sending Well*, "Develop Great Coaches," creates ten simple targets for coaches who want to move their coaching from okay to great. At the end of each chapter is a checklist to evaluate your coaching as it relates to the quality and to help you determine steps forward to grow into a great coach.

 **CHAPTER 5**

The Serving Coach

Ken,

Thanks for making time for our conversation on Wednesday. We touched on a number of issues, including your time with Greg, the ongoing development of equipping your leaders, and measuring progress in the four goals you've identified. We also talked about improving communications. Perhaps we can drill down on the communications issue during our next conversation on December 2.

See you tomorrow!

Kim

Great Coaching Is Not about You

If Rick Warren wrote a book about coaching, his "It's not about you"[1] opening would work again. Coaching improves when coaches learn principles like this one: Great coaching is not about your ability or your résumé.

Great coaching is about wrapping a towel around your waist, getting on the floor, and washing the dirty feet of another disciple.

James and John never read *The Purpose Driven Life*, but it might have helped if they had. In a moment of honesty, they fueled a controversy on Jesus' leadership team. James and John requested top positions in Jesus' new government. This request was all about them. Jesus responded to the request of James and John by explaining His path to greatness:

> "But it shall not be so among you. But whoever would be great among you must be your servant, and whoever would be first among you must be slave of all. For even the Son of Man came not to be served but to serve, and to give his life as a ransom for many." (Mark 10:43–45)

The Serving Coach understands his rank in the kingdom hierarchy. The pathway to great coaching involves a dramatic heart shift. The Serving Coach is waiting on tables, willing to go unrecognized, and dying to self for the sake of a church planter's unique kingdom assignment. Obedience motivates the Serving Coach. How does this look?

Falling out of Love Is the First Step

As a new coach, I struggled in the same ways most new coaches do. I loved the idea of coaching and had benefited incredibly by being coached. Coaching made sense, but the voices in my head pushed against my coaching skills.

> Great coaching is about wrapping a towel around your waist, getting on the floor, and washing the dirty feet of another disciple.

I was aware that I had the right solutions for the people I "coached," but it was against the rules to give the solutions. I would lock my jaws tight and practice my new discipline.

An important turning point in my coaching journey was the day I fell out of love with my advice. The advice-giving voice in my head that was secretly giving solutions got weaker. And my coaching became better and more authentic.

Coach trainer and writer Keith Webb chronicles his evolution from advisor to aspiring coach to coach in his book *The*

COACH Model® for Christian Leaders. As a supervisor of church planters in both Japan and Indonesia, he experienced the tension of his approach.

With all good intentions, Keith directed and advised missionaries for whom he was responsible. His results were mixed at best, particularly in the beginning. When he made the transition to Indonesia, he was practicing coaching principles, but the stakes changed. Indonesian leaders took advice from someone above them seriously. Every detail was followed exactly. But they were also living out the gospel in an Islamic country that was resistant. The advice they followed could result in arrest, torture, or death.[2]

That was a turning point for Keith:

> Each person and team needed to hear from the Holy Spirit regarding his or her next steps. If the Holy Spirit directed them to go somewhere or to do something that resulted in persecution, then that was God's will. It was critical that they heard from God, not from me.[3]

Coaching is about what God wants for the lives of the church planters we serve—it is not about us.

Willingness to Ask Tough Questions Is the Next Step

Another important transition for a coach is the willingness to ask tough questions. The asking transition is not an easy one. The transition is from the position of a talker who drives the conversation to the position of a listener who receives the conversation. Bob Logan's personal advice to me spoke a language I understood best as a former baseball player:

Be a catcher, not a pitcher.

As God moves deeper into the life of the planter you coach, something unique happens. How liberating for the servant-coach to operate with the full confidence that he can never ultimately fix the person he coaches, but God can. Coaches serve by being present for the process and asking great questions. Here are four examples of great questions asked by my coaches:

1. What does the Father think about what you are doing?

THE AWARENESS QUESTION (JOHN BAILEY)

My friend, John Bailey, stopped me in my tracks one day with a question. He was coaching me through the minutia of an event I was planning. He served me by reminding me of the presence of God in my life and ministry. John asked, "What does the Father think about what you are doing?" My honest first response was, "That has not crossed my mind." But John's question helped me pause and view my activities for God from God's perspective.

Serving Coach Question:

How can coaches help people be aware of the presence of God in the coaching moment?

2. How can you create new scoreboards?

THE RUT QUESTION (BILL HOWARD)

Many people you coach are stuck. When my former pastor and coach asked me, "How can you created new scoreboards?" I was stuck. I was trying to create radically new habits with an old mindset. In essence, I told him, "I was successful at this when I had different scoreboards, but I am not motivated without the old scoreboards."

Serving Coach Question:

How can coaches help people establish fresh perspectives on lifelong struggles?

3. What is drawing you to these areas?

THE HEART QUESTION (RYAN KNEPP)

We all want to do the right things, but if we don't want to do them for the right reasons, success will be temporary. I told my coach for the day, Ryan Knepp, a church planter from Pennsylvania, that I wanted to be more effective at home, church, and in my city. Good intentions, right? Of course.

But Ryan challenged me with this question: "What is drawing you to these areas?" The question did not seem confrontational, but as a great coach, Ryan refused to assume. Great coaches target the heart, not merely the behavior or intent.

Serving Coach Question:

How can we help people discover the deeper motivation of their hearts?

4. What is your best thinking to date?

THE RESPONSIBILITY QUESTION (BOB LOGAN)

We are always looking to get ministry advice from qualified advisors. But we should avoid becoming addicted to the advice of others. When Bob Logan (who was a highly qualified advisor) was my coach, I was sure he knew the hidden secrets to my ministry success. I grew quite familiar with his most common response when I asked for advice: "What is your best thinking to date?" I discovered that I had to grow past the first-level question: "What would Bob do?" More challenging questions like "What does God want?" and "What should I do?" were an important part of my growth.

Serving Coach Question:

How can I help people overcome an advice addiction to grow?

As God develops you as a coach, you will move from trying to memorize great questions to coaching in the moment. In your next coaching conversation, listen with strong curiosity and a heart to serve. Trust God to lead you. On your quest to advance as a Serving Coach, consider the following five practices.

Five Practices of the Serving Coach

Practice 1: I connect with planters I coach between coaching conversations.

> As God develops you as a coach, you will move from trying to memorize great questions to coaching in the moment.

Building trust is the key to a healthy, life-giving coaching relationship. Trust grows when a planter sees the relationship as more than a ministry task to you.

Don't overwhelm your planter with a deluge of communication. The last thing he needs is a stalker. But be intentional about how you connect. Most connections will require more intentionality than time. Here are ten ways you can connect with the planters you coach between coaching conversations:

1. Send a relevant article, quote, or blog.
2. Text before an important event expressing your prayer support.
3. Send a book via an online book distributer.
4. Acknowledge special occasions like birthdays, anniversaries, etc.
5. Send an email reminder of previous action items.
6. Attend a meeting or conference together.
7. Recreate together.
8. Send a gift card.
9. Meet for lunch or coffee.
10. Attend a special event at his church.

Practice 2: I ask how I can improve my coaching.

Every person I coach is unique. Not only are they unique as individuals, but they are also different from me. When you look at the list below, you will discover an incredible number of variables that provide more unique combinations than Starbucks.

We previously asked a brainstorming question during our one-day coach orientation to reinforce this important reality of coaching: *How are church planters unique?* Here are examples:

Personality	Strengths	Weaknesses
Experiences	Preferences	Spiritual Gifts
Family History	Education	Spiritual History
Passions	Birthplace	Places Lived
Culture	Ethnicity	Generation
Home Life	Physical Health	Mental Health
Emotional Health	Church Background	
	Body Type	

When you add the unique context and timing of their plant along with core group, etc., the combinations continue to multiply exponentially.

What is the point? Never assume that your coaching is connecting with the planter you coach. Every coaching relationship is unique. You may have internationally recognized coaching credentials, but that does not make your next relationship or conversation a guaranteed success.

Evaluating the coaching relationship and conversations belongs under any of the ten qualities of a great coach. But the Serving Coach communicates an important message with his ongoing monitoring of his coaching. Coaching is all about serving the unique needs and challenges of the planter.

Give the person you coach choices to help him give you feedback. "How is my coaching for you? Too easy? Too tough? Just right?" If you tend to be an easy coach, you will likely get permission to press harder. If you are too tough, you may need to back off. But most important, keep asking. You will communicate an important message to those you serve: "This relationship is not about me."

Practice 3: I send follow-up emails after our meetings with action items and highlights.

This chapter began with an example of a follow-up email. At times, you may feel like an administrative assistant as opposed to a coach. But always remember you are here to serve. Maybe that is what your planter needs most. Taking good notes and sending follow-up emails are important. Planters will appreciation a summary of the coaching conversation from your perspective.

Here are three tips to writing an effective follow-up email:

1. *Do it fast.* The conversation and to-do list are fresh on your mind. Compose it immediately after the call is over. If I don't send it immediately, odds are I never will.
2. *Take coaching notes in a ready-to-send email.* This tip is gold. A few minutes of editing, point, and shoot.
3. *Write in a bulleted format.* My follow-up emails were narratives that included actual dialogue in the past. That created too much to read and too much to write. The planter doesn't want my coaching epistle. Keep it short.

Encourage your planter to capture notes and details as well. I often include in my summary email: "Here are some notes to add to yours." For the planter you coach to benefit, he needs to own the process fully. The planter needs to outwork the coach for effective coaching. If not, the relationship can turn into something dysfunctional and unproductive quickly.

Here are five advantages of sending a follow-up email:

1. The importance of the conversation is reinforced.
2. The value of coaching is enhanced.
3. A note-taking discipline is modeled.
4. Coaching details are stored for easy access.
5. The planter is served.

Using strong online coaching tools like *CoachNet* (www. coachnet.org) and *My Coaching Log* (www.mycoachlog.com) can meet the need for capturing good notes with minimal effort. I have used and benefited from both.

Practice 4: I calendar multiple meetings in advance.

I received a phone call years ago from a church planter and close friend. He explained an opportunity he was offered to have a coach. He then presented me an easy question: "Do I really have time to be coached?" My response was, "You don't have time not to be coached."

Coaching helps planters manage time more effectively. Great coaching will produce clarity and accountability that will help you get better results in day-to-day projects. The demands come at planters so quickly that choosing what is important is virtually impossible.

To add another couple of meetings a month to the schedule of a planter or a coach is daunting. Without a 100-percent commitment by both, effective coaching will never happen. Great intentions do not produce great coaching. Here are ways to make calendaring work:

1. Schedule a meeting to calendar the meetings. I have followed this principle for years. During our one-day coach orientation, we ask coaches to schedule four peer-coaching meetings before they leave and return the schedule to us. The meetings will never happen if they don't.

2. Agree to reschedule immediately in case of an emergency cancellation. Life happens, but cancellations between busy people are avoidable. When they happen, reschedule immediately—the same week if possible. When you are overwhelmed with busyness is when you need to meet with your coach the most.

3. Choose a standing appointment. "Every other Friday at noon for the next four months" removes all the guesswork and scheduling complexities. Negotiate with the planter you coach for ideal times that have a greater possibility to happen.

The value of coaching increases based on two factors: how *often* you meet and how *many times* you meet. If you are not meeting consistently with the planter you coach, then you are not serving him well. Neither are you modeling the elements of a great coaching relationship.

Practice 5: I plan twenty minutes before and after a meeting for prep, prayer, review, and evaluation.

The Serving Coach is committed to doing whatever it takes to serve. He creates systems and utilizes best practices to serve efficiently. For example, I write the names of family members and interesting facts about them on large index cards. Those cards prompt my memory during coaching conversations and become flashcards to help me memorize important data.

Strong Hellos and Goodbyes

Strong hellos and goodbyes have always been keys to strong relationships. The way you start and end coaching conversations is a secret to great coaching. Start your conversations three to four days in advance by sending a series of open-ended questions to the planter you coach.

Strong Hellos

1. *Preparation (ten minutes).* Two things are needed to get the most out of a limited prep time: the follow-up email from your last conversation and the answered prep questions for the current conversation. I suggest you print both to be able to prepare more quickly and use both pages during the coaching time. Use the answers sent by the planter to write follow-up questions.

2. *Prayer (ten minutes):* You have ten minutes to talk to the Father about what He wants in today's conversation. You can review the answers before Him and pray that you would serve your planter well. Pray that the Holy Spirit will lead you to all truth and that the planter will hear and obey God's voice.

Strong Goodbyes

3. *Review (ten minutes):* Carefully review your notes and send your follow-up email. Preparation has now started for the next coaching conversation. Great job!

4. *Evaluation (ten minutes):* Your performance as a coach is the same as your performance in any other skill. You will have good days and bad days. But we have provided a "Great Coaching Checklist" to help you debrief in Appendix H. This checklist will help you coach yourself through the highs and lows of your coaching. To self-evaluate is to serve the next planter you coach. And you will move one step closer to becoming a great coach.

Check the statements that best describe your coaching.

	The Practices of the Serving Coach
	I connect with planters between coaching conversations.
	I ask planters how I can improve my coaching for them.
	I send follow-up emails after our meetings with action items and highlights.
	I calendar multiple coaching meetings in advance.
	I plan twenty minutes before and after a coaching call for prep, prayer, review, and evaluation.

Be Coached . . .

1. What *could* you do to grow in this quality?

2. What *will* you do to grow in this quality?

3. Who could help you?

My Coach Helps . . .

As a planter, I can attest to the benefit that my coaching relationships have had on me personally and on my ministry. With a few good questions, my coaches have helped me to focus, gain perspective, and push through issues that could easily have been roadblocks. Some of my most productive seasons of ministry have been those times when I had a coach walking with me.

Jason McGibbon
The Hamilton Fellowships
Hamilton, Ontario Canada
www.facebook.com/jason.mcgibbon.5

The Serving Coach

Serving and giving are core coaching practices. Coaches enjoy helping others win. Jesus' mission was to serve and give: "'For even the Son of Man came not to be served but to serve, and to give his life as a ransom for many'" (Mark 10:45).

 **CHAPTER 6**

The Believing Coach

"Ambition is attractive, but calling is irresistible. God has made it unmistakably clear that He is calling us to plant a church in Portland—and it's already been an incredible journey," said Aaron Bennett. Aaron and Andrea Bennett put their "yes" on the table and in a step of bold faith moved from Georgia to plant Spring of Life Church in Portland, Oregon (www.springoflifepdx.com).

Aaron attended new coach orientation near the beginning of his journey—and he was hooked. Though no stranger to mentoring others in ministry, Aaron had a lightbulb moment when the group discussed how coaching is different from advising, teaching, counseling, and mentoring. He knew he wanted to coach and be coached.

And the timing couldn't have been better. Aaron was on the cusp of a new church plant in the heart of downtown Portland "inviting thirsty people to become disciples of Jesus." Aaron and his wife, Andrea, say that "Portland represents an amazing gospel opportunity."

When asked about how coaching has supported their early church planting efforts, Aaron quickly pointed to tangible details. He talked about how his coach helped him follow through on easy-to-overlook aspects of hosting summer mission teams: "The frequency of the coaching conversations makes me know I'm accountable to follow up on those things I wanted to do. My coach didn't tell me to do them. I'm the one that said that these are the things God has placed before me and in my heart."

Bold Faith Needed

Planters need bold faith like Aaron and Andrea's to plant a church. Their coaches need bold faith as well. "Church planting gives you one of the greatest opportunities to see God work on your behalf in miraculous ways," according to Mac Lake, senior director of Planter Development of the Send Network.[1]

Skill and experience are not as important as what a coach believes about the planter he coaches. People will test your confidence. All of us have tested the confidence of our mentors, coaches, and teachers. Anybody we coach can disappoint us. But at that point, our coaching influence is neutralized.

As coaches, we will place our faith in something or someone. We believe in something. But we can believe in the wrong thing without knowing it. Our best intentions can crowd God out of the picture. Below are five wrong beliefs.

Five Wrong Coaching Beliefs

1. We believe in the person.

We do planters no favors by believing in them. Too much confidence in planters can sabotage the coaching relationship. *Here are the unintended outcomes:*

- The planter tries to please the coach.
- The coach tries to please the planter.
- Planters avoid transparency.
- Planters become self-reliant.

Great coaches shift their cheering language to avoid references to themselves. For example, affirmations like "I love it" or "I think you are doing great," though well intended, are pointed in the wrong direction. Change the "I" cheering to "You" cheering. For example, "You are doing great right now at developing small group leaders" or "You are leading your church to connect well with the community." "God is working in you."

Planters need faith to pursue what God has invited them to do. If coaches place too much confidence in planters, we help them move their focus away from God and to themselves. Disappointment is sure to follow.

"Multiply" is one of the church planter training paths of the Send Network. "Bold Faith: Leading with a Faith that Takes Prayerful Risks" is one of Multiply's 12 Leadership Competencies. Mac Lake warns planters:

> One of the biggest temptations planters face is self-reliance. They hear from God and get excited about the Vision of God, but then they stop listening to the Voice of God. Before they know it, they find themselves saying, "I don't know what to do next."[2]

2. We believe in coaching.

Coaching is a different approach to develop and empower leaders. But like any new approach, the approach can get the attention. Coaching is what we do, but it can never be why we exist—or the belief behind the action.

In my early days of coaching, no one in my world was safe. I was fascinated by the prospect of listening to people. What a novel way to serve someone else! In the past, I thought my expertise was all I had to offer. Now, the pressure to give brilliant advice was off. The conversations with everyone I coached became more interesting and productive. God gave me a solution through the simple vehicle of coaching to listen better and to help leaders more effectively.

Can you imagine what would happen if every citizen in the kingdom became a coach? There would be lots of people asking questions and listening for answers, but no answers. Coaches should remain aware that coaching is an imperfect vehicle provided by an imperfect person to help leaders do a perfect God's will.

3. We believe in quick fixes.

Great coaching involves intentional, long-term investments. Over time, the conversations will get tougher, as will the challenges church planters face. Great coaches take risks to point out blind spots, contradictions, and repeated patterns. Great coaching takes time.

> Great coaching involves intentional, long-term investments.

We created a simple, minimalist approach to coaching planters that values the relationship first. How often and how many times a coach meets with a planter are most important. A great coach who seldom meets with his planter, or meets in short bursts before milestone church planting events, is less valuable than the steady investor.

The most competent and credible coaches normally have the least discretionary time. The investment is high to coach a planter, so our expectation of where church planter coaches invest their time is critical.

4. We believe in our stories.

I was doing a live coaching demonstration with my friend Ray in Vancouver. Ray clarified his objective for the coaching conversation. "My mother is in a nursing home in Texas," Ray explained. At that point, I made an immediate emotional connection with Ray. My mother was also in a nursing home. As a fellow pastor and son, I wanted to console Ray. I wanted him to know I understood what he was facing and offer him advice from my experience that might help him.

I was learning about the potential negative effect of comparing stories during coaching conversations, so I resisted the urge to tell my story. Another urge is to make this coaching conversation about my situation so Ray could help me. But this conversation was not about me. This conversation was about Ray, his needs, and his unique situation.

We patiently walked together through Ray's challenges, and he established action steps to follow. But in hearing Ray's story, a powerful lesson was reinforced. The only thing in common about our stories was part of his opening sentence, "My mother is in a nursing home . . ." Had I hijacked the conversation with my story, Ray would have missed the moment.

If I needed coaching or counseling time with Ray about my mother, he would have served me gladly. But this was Ray's time, his story, and, more importantly, God's story. Guard against merging stories to save time, particularly during formal coaching conversations. Your next formal coaching conversation is not about you.

5. We believe in our success formulas.

Most of us have a difficult time forgetting our own fruitfulness. Try as we may to give God credit, our human tendency is to believe that our past fruitfulness provides a path for all those who come behind us.

Learning from the successes of others has value. But at what point do our success stories overshadow God's timely intervention? When we miss this point, leaders have no other option but to imitate the steps of another leader in hopes of getting the same results.

> Most of us have a difficult time forgetting our own fruitfulness.

The story behind any success story is "Look what God did!" The hero of every kingdom success story is God, not ourselves. Coaches with confidence in God's ability to transform people or circumstances say, "How God will succeed through you will be different, but He will. What He has done, He will do again."

When God miraculously intervenes in the life of a planter, changing his heart, behavior, or situation, the Believing Coach takes a stone and places it there. The stone becomes a testimony and a reminder of the faithfulness of God. When God changes lives through a planter's church, the Believing Coach repeats the discipline. Revisiting those stones together will be invaluable faith builders in the future.

Coaching Is a Faith Partnership

Coaching is co-believers walking together for a season of obedience to Jesus. The coach is encouraged by the dynamic calling of the planter and his family. The planter is encouraged by the faith story and the active faith of the coach. Paul described this faith dynamic between co-believers:

> *Coaching is co-believers walking together for a season of obedience to Jesus.*

For I long to see you, that I may impart to you some spiritual gift to strengthen you—that is, that we may be mutually encouraged by each other's faith, both yours and mine. (Rom. 1:11–12)

The Believing Coach is careful not to misplace his faith in the planter's abilities, although he may respect them. The Believing Coach sees God at work in the planting process. On your quest to advance as a Believing Coach, consider the following five practices.

Five Practices of the Believing Coach

Practice 1: I experience the transforming power of Christ in my life.

My first babysitter's bathroom was a wooden shack a little bigger than a phone booth in a field behind her house. The whole experience terrified me as a three-year-old, but that little shack was important to all of us. Besides the sights, sounds, and smells inside the little shack, do you know the image I will never forget? The path to the shack was as hard as concrete, and nothing ever grew on it. You know why? Because people walked the same direction every day for years.

This image reminds me of the four reminders Believing Coaches need.

1. Look for new ground in your walk with Christ. Leaders and coaches struggle when challenging people to go places we are not going ourselves. Our successes and cheers from our biggest fans cause us to repeat the past. Inside we can be stuck while outside all seems well. The path is like concrete. Find a new path.

2. Don't confuse spiritual growth with your development as a leader. You can develop your skills of communication, productivity, and organizational leadership, yet fail to develop spiritually. Be aware of the difference and make yourself accountable to someone.

3. Be open about your need to grow. Make your struggles visible, particularly for those in your inner circle. Be vulnerable. Then, when God grows you, tell that story. Your story will be believable because they saw it happen before their very own eyes.

4. Be in community with people who help you. To whom are you accountable? Who asks you the tough questions? Who encourages you? Who is your coach? Who pushes you? What are your growth goals for this year?

Romans 12:2 answers a transformational question: What does God want?

> Do not be conformed to this world, but be transformed by the renewal of your mind, that by testing you may discern what is the will of God, what is good and acceptable and perfect. (Rom. 12:2)

God's remaking process in our lives never ends. It goes beyond our ministry skills to how we live as disciples.

Practice 2: I ask transformational questions.

The Believing Coach holds up a mirror to the planter so he sees himself more closely. Part of his focus is asking transformational questions. For example:

- Who are you becoming?
- How are you growing?
- What does God want?
- What is God saying?
- What needs to change?
- What is really happening?
- How is God changing you?
- Where are you resisting change?
- Where are you stuck?
- What are you avoiding?
- What are your fears?
- What is your priority?

God used my first coaches to change the way I approached life and ministry. Did I accomplish new projects and initiatives? Of course. Did I see immediate results in getting things done? Yes. But those momentary wins helped me discover new approaches to everything.

Coaching is a tool of God to transform a leader by touching every area of his life. Everyone in their lives sees the change. The Believing Coach wants to see God help people for the month, the year, and for life.

Why ask transformational questions?
- Because coaches help planters endure.
- Because coaches are part of God's ongoing formation process.
- Because coaches help planters obey publicly and privately.
- Because coaches go deeper than the project of the month.
- Because coaches help planters take responsibility for what is happening.

How do I improve at asking transformational questions?
- By learning how a transformational question is different.
- By practicing transformational questions with a friend.

- By finding great transformational questions used by others.
- By creating your own transformational questions.
- By evaluating how often you ask transformational questions.

When do I ask transformational questions?
- When prompted by the Holy Spirit.
- When I am more acquainted with the planter.
- When I see a planter blaming others.
- When all coaching conversations focus on the church.
- When I see a planter struggling.

Practice 3: I coach the planter, not the plant.

Helping a planter manage his projects and problems is a positive outcome of coaching. However, if all your meetings are about projects and problems, you are missing the full potential of coaching. The planter may be more productive and see better results but miss something deeper God wants to do.

Transformational questions are different from "now" questions. Both types of questions have value, but there is a distinct difference between the two. Transformational questions focus on God's transforming process in the planter.

Now Questions	Transformational Questions
Do	Be
Circumstances	Person
Skills	Character
Urgent	Enduring
External	Internal
Outside	Personal
Easier	More Challenging
Execution	Maturity
What's next?	What are your struggles?
What would you like to work on today?	What does God want?
What's urgent?	What is God saying?

Practice 4: I coach beyond symptoms to heart issues.

Imagine calling your doctor to tell him or her you are in terrible pain. Would you expect a reputable doctor to say, "Well let's get you some pain medication quickly?" Of course not. A good doctor sees pain as a *symptom*. A well-intended interrogation process begins:

- Where is the pain?
- How long have you been in pain?
- How severe is your pain?
- How have you addressed the pain?
- What other symptoms are you experiencing?

Your next step is an office visit. Have you ever noticed how many questions you face when making a doctor visit? From parking lot to parking lot and at all points in between, questions like "Who? What? When? How often? Where?" are directed at you.

Pain may be a warning of something life threatening, but it is always a symptom of something else. Pain is never the problem. Your doctor wants to relieve your pain by discovering the actual source of the pain. The process will continue until the source is discovered.

The Believing Coach resists the temptation to help a planter relieve pain. He coaches beyond symptoms to the source. The source is the heart:

Guard your heart above all else, for it determines the course of your life. (Prov. 4:23 NLT)

May the words of my mouth and the meditation of my heart be pleasing to you, O Lord, my rock and my redeemer. (Ps. 19:14 NLT)

Wherever your treasure is, there the desires of your heart will also be. (Matt. 6:21 NLT)

Generosity is a heart issue. Conflict, participation, and neighboring concerns are heart concerns. Here are some examples of the shift:

> **Question (Now):** How can you convince people to be more generous?
>
> **Better Question (Transformational):** How can you address the heart issues that influence generosity?

> **Question (Now):** How can you increase small group attendance?
>
> **Better Question (Transformational):** How can you address the heart issues that cause people to avoid community?

Symptoms initiate a healthy discovery process. The discoveries may reveal life-threatening problems or simple problems. What's happening inside the planter? What's happening inside the planter's family? What's happening inside the disciples in development? What's going on inside the church? Transformational questions help develop a hopeful leader who leads from the heart.

Practice 5: I view the planter I coach through a biblical lens.

The Believing Coach has a God-inspired optimism that embraces the fact that "in Christ" people have unlimited potential. Keep the statements and Scripture near the place you normally coach. They will remind you of biblical realities about the person you are coaching. Also, use these passages in your coaching to affirm your planter.

1. God is speaking to the planter I am coaching.

"My sheep hear my voice, and I know them, and they follow me" (John 10:27).

- What story can you tell about when you clearly heard God?
- Where do you need to hear from God now?

2. The Holy Spirit lives inside the planter I am coaching.

"You know him, for he dwells with you and will be in you" (John 14:17).

- What is the most important lesson you have learned about the Holy Spirit?
- How can you apply the lesson to your current situation?

3. God has gifted the planter I am coaching.

"As each has received a gift, use it to serve one another" (1 Pet. 4:10).

- What are your spiritual gifts?
- What can you do to operate more in your gifted areas?

4. Jesus has invited the planter I am coaching on a journey with Him.

"Follow me, and I will make you fishers of men" (Matt. 4:19).

- What is the most encouraging part of what you are doing for Jesus?
- What is the most memorable part of your call to planting?

5. God at work in the person I am coaching.

"For it is God who works in you, both to will and to work for his good pleasure" (Phil. 2:13).

- How has God changed you over the last year?
- What is He is changing in you now?

Coaching is a faith partnership. Planters need bold faith. And planters need coaches who have bold faith. The Believing Coach places his faith solely in God's ability. He is a gift from God to a planter.

The Believing Coach

What drives a great coach is the core belief in God's ability to change people. Paul's encouraging words serve as the lens through which coaches see the planters they coach: "And I am sure of this, that he who began a good work in you will bring it to completion at the day of Jesus Christ" (Phil. 1:6).

Check the statements that best describe your coaching.

	The Practices of the Believing Coach
	I experience the transforming power of Christ in my life.
	I ask transformational questions.
	I coach the planter, not the plant.
	I coach beyond symptoms.
	I view the planter I coach through a biblical lens.

Be Coached . . .

1. What *could* you do to grow in this quality?

2. What *will* you do to grow in this quality?

3. Who could help you?

My Coach Helps . . .

My coach helps me process through difficult decisions and next steps. He has helped me think through the most critical and pressing issues that need to be addressed. He helps me analyze the situation and leave with actionable items. I respect my coach a lot, and he has helped me get through very difficult times in the church plant.

Bobby Wood
Redemption Church
Ogden, Utah
www.redemptionutah.com

 **CHAPTER 7**

The Listening Coach

JD and Natalie Mangrum moved to Boston to plant their second church. JD's first church planter coach was Ed Cerny. Ed is a professional coach, former marketing professor, and has been on the leadership team in two Myrtle Beach church plants. We tell more of Ed's side of church planter coaching in chapter 13. Here is John's perspective on how Ed helped him:

> Ed was a great coach because he spoke wisdom and pointed me to books or habits. But even more, he showed me what a life of faith looks like. He cared for me over and over again. At the birth of my children, the death of my father, every birthday and anniversary, long after the formal coaching process concluded, Ed would write, call, or email to encourage.
>
> In a church planting season of wanting answers, Ed provided questions. Rather than challenging me to get answers from someone else's victories, he asked the right questions so I would chart my own course. He helped me learn that what God called me to do, He would equip me to do. He delighted in my discovery rather than gaining credit from giving easy answers. Invaluable!
>
> Ed was the best. He walked with me through forgiving my dad at the height of his lostness while we were planting the church. Then when my dad unexpectedly gave his life to Jesus and died of a massive heart attack hours later, Ed

grieved and celebrated. This was five years *after* his coaching responsibilities were concluded.

JD's story is a case study about how great coaching looks. JD's perspective about how great coaching influenced him as a disciple and planter is noteworthy. Imagine the hours of communication between Ed and JD over the years. How would the story be different if Ed had been impatient and anxious to get JD to do things his way?

The First Time I Ever Listened

I was celebrating my twenty-fifth wedding anniversary when I took my coaching practice to a dangerous new level. I had spent the previous twelve months going through some incredible training processes, and I was determined to coach everything that breathed. I decided to offer my wife, Yvette, a short coaching session while we were sitting on the beach in Hilton Head, South Carolina. It felt as awkward to me as it did to her—but I knew I needed to practice, and I thought she needed to know what all the buzz was about.

As I wrapped up the coaching conversation, I asked, "What do you think?" She replied, "We have been married twenty-five years, and I think this is the first time you've ever really listened to me."

I got high marks on my coaching practice session but a low grade on being a good husband!

Jesus on Listening

Jesus invited His disciples into a relationship, not a business agreement. Hours, days, and years of communication were involved. Jesus modeled the love, patience, and gentleness of an expert listener.

Think about the master class Jesus gives on listening in the Gospels. You will discover numerous examples of Jesus the listener. Here are three: the rich young ruler, the woman at the well, and the woman caught in adultery. Each of these people had unique barriers to understanding Him, but Jesus attempted to understand them first by listening and asking questions. And as He engaged them, they were able to understand themselves better. Here are three observations about listening:

1. Listening is a learned response.

None of us were born listeners; all of us were born waiting and ready to talk. Listening takes practice and a desire to care for people. Only Jesus was the master listener. We will be lifelong apprentices in the craft of listening.

> Jesus invited His disciples into a relationship, not a business agreement.

2. Listening is a spiritual discipline.

Jesus modeled ideal listening and asking skills. Spiritual disciplines are part of following Jesus. When you listen, you esteem others better than yourself. When you listen, you honor others. When you listen, you grow in Christ. Every believer should practice the spiritual discipline of listening.

3. Listening is the fruit of godly character.

"But the Holy Spirit produces this kind of fruit in our lives: love, joy, peace, patience, kindness, goodness, faithfulness, gentleness, and self-control" (Gal. 5:22–23 NLT). Review each kind of fruit listed. How does the fruit of *love* make a better listener? Continue asking the same question about each kind of fruit. Every fruit listed above would contribute to making a great listener.

> When you listen, you honor others.

Jesus on Asking

Great listeners ask great questions. Listening and asking are inseparable. Curiosity creates a desire in a listener to go deeper. Jesus was not only a great listener; He was also, according to Martin Copenhaver, a great questioner:

Jesus is a questioner. Jesus is not the ultimate Answer Man—He is more like the Great Questioner. Jesus asks more questions than He is asked. In the four Gospels Jesus asks 307 different questions. By contrast, He is only asked 183 questions.[1]

Out of the 307 questions Jesus asked, we have plenty to learn about asking and listening. Here are three examples.

1. "What do you want me to do for you?" (Matt. 20:32)

This question is clarifying. Jesus asked this question of two blind men who asked Him for mercy. If the intended objective isn't clarified, then a path forward is unclear. Jesus knew what they wanted and needed, yet He asked the question anyway. He wanted them to understand the solution to their deepest longings. Give the planter you coach a great question and listen closely to their response. Over time, you will learn their deepest longings. For example: "What can I do to help you today?"

2. "What is written in the Law? How do you read it?" (Luke 10:26)

This question is establishing. Jesus is teaching the parable of the Good Samaritan. A lawyer, who is well versed in the facts, is asking him questions. Jesus, as a listener, directs him to the facts. Ask the planter you coach a question that leads him back to truth. For example: "What is true? How does God's Word address your question?"

> Give the planter you coach the gift of a compelling question related to his goals and challenges.

3. "Do you believe this?" (John 11:26)

This question is compelling. Jesus had just returned from Bethany at the request of His friends, Mary and Martha. His friend and their brother, Lazarus, was dead. Jesus, at that moment, reminded Martha that He is the "resurrection and the life." Rather than scolding her for not believing, He asked her, "Do you believe this?" In her moment of turmoil, Martha must have felt the weight of this question. Give the planter you coach the gift of a compelling question related to his goals and challenges. For example, "How confident are you that God can do this for you? Do you believe that this is possible?"

Asking questions is at the heart of what it means to be a good listener. Discipline and the fruit of the Spirit are required. On your quest to advance as a Listening Coach, consider the following five practices.

Five Practices of the Listening Coach

Practice 1: I coach in a listening environment free from distractions.

Inspired by the advice that candles create calm working environments, I decided to take action. Calm is not my default, so I thought it was worth a try. A small, scented candle now burned on my desk during my workday.

As I turned a page of my notes during a coaching call, my calm, distraction-free coaching environment went up in flames as a result of my scented candle. Even better, this was a video call, so my friend Woody was able to see, hear, and experience how a distracted coach looks. Sometimes my life does serve as a warning to others—and provides a few laughs along the way. You may have days like that as well.

Our world is designed to distract us: texts, social media, blogs, notifications, and phone calls. And that's just the last ten minutes! We distract ourselves with concerns, plans, ideas, and bad coaching environments. And in spite of our best efforts, distractions will happen.

Great coaching demands listening well, and listening well requires a distraction-free environment. The writer of Proverbs admonishes: "Let your eyes look directly forward, and your gaze be straight before you" (Prov. 4:25).

Most of these suggestions can apply to video, phone, or face-to-face meetings. To minimize distractions, try these tips:

- Use a quiet area for your coaching conversations. Coffee shops or homes full of active people and pets are not ideal.
- Never coach while driving.
- Learn the locations of your strongest cell and Internet connections.
- Use quality ear buds to minimize outside noise.
- Avoid multitasking during your coaching conversations.
- Take twenty minutes before the conversation to focus your attention.
- Don't answer your phone during those twenty minutes.
- Turn all computer and phone notifications off.
- Don't check email during a coaching conversation.
- Enable an auto-reply message for incoming texts or emails.
- Pray—for focus, clarity, and wisdom.

And remember—great coaching is a work in progress. If a particular coaching conversation gets derailed due to distractions, be persistent. Make adjustments and try again.

Practice 2: I summarize back what I hear planters saying.

Any conversation has the potential for misunderstanding. We experience this all the time in marriage, parenting, and ministry. Perhaps you've come away from a deep conversation thinking you understood what the other person said, only to later realize they meant something altogether different. It's all too easy to assume we understand what we hear.

Understanding is crucial to listening well. Misunderstanding what the person being coached is saying may cause us to ask questions that are neither relevant nor helpful. One great way to avoid this pitfall is to summarize back to the person I'm coaching what I hear him saying:

What I hear you saying is that you are feeling overwhelmed by the logistics of Sunday morning services and that you would like to explore ways to reduce this stress. Is that correct? How would you like to expand on that?

Be sure you pause after you summarize. This verification is invaluable if done well. The planter gets a chance to reflect on what he said and either confirm the direction or redirect the conversation. Summarizing during a coaching conversation helps keep the conversation on track and helps the planter know you are listening.

> Coaching helps draw out the real issues through the use of probing follow-up questions.

Practice 3: I ask follow-up questions based on the previous answers.

Coaching helps church planters work through problems. But sometimes the problems are not so obvious. Coaching helps draw out the real issues through the use of probing follow-up questions.

Your next (and best) questions are always found in what the planter you are coaching just said. Listen between the lines. Be on alert for what God is doing in the heart of the storyteller. Here are some examples to help you probe deeper as you listen well:

- What did you mean when you said _____?
- How did _____ change your direction or perspective?
- Why did you say _____?
- When did _____ happen? How did that timing impact you?
- How do you feel now about _____?
- What is God saying about _____?

Be curious about what your church planter is saying, and you'll get your next questions from him!

Practice 4: I take notes during my coaching conversations.

Details of the coaching conversation may be lost if we do not write them down or use digital note-taking methods. Taking notes during coaching conversations is part of great coaching. Tell the planter you're coaching that you are taking notes. Note-taking demonstrates that you are interested and invested in the coaching process. You don't have to write down everything verbatim; bullet points, highlights, and short quotes help you ask deeper questions and remember details. Your notes also provide the basis for your follow-up email after the coaching conversation ends.

Note-taking can be done on your computer, tablet, or with a notebook and pen. Find a note-taking method that is not distracting, and that helps you stay engaged in the process.

Practice 5: I talk no more than 20 percent of the time.

John Whitmore said, "Perhaps the hardest thing a coach has to learn to do is to shut up!"[2]

James wrote the same advice with a kinder, gentler tone:

Understand this, my dear brothers and sisters: You must all be quick to listen, slow to speak, and slow to get angry. (James 1:19 NLT)

I hope anger will not be a huge temptation in your coaching conversations, but talking too much certainly will be.

Listening is an acquired skill and a spiritual discipline. Practice is the first step. Steve Nicolson and Jeff Bailey, in their book, *Coaching Church Planters*, say this about listening:

. . . Most people (including pastors) are not good at listening to others; preoccupation with our own thoughts and opinions, coupled with a compulsion to talk—particularly if one is placed in any kind of advisory role—is strong. *Listening is a skill requiring intentional concentration and practice.*[3]

This "20 percent" rule is so easy to violate in coaching—we love being heard. But so does your planter, and that is why you are coaching in the first place. Yours is one of the rare relationships God has given him. Listening is on the top of your agenda. Always err on the side of listening more and talking less. Our advice is less helpful than we think, and the Holy Spirit is at work in the planters you coach, speaking His truth to their hearts and minds.

Below are four ideas to help you monitor your talking and listening while coaching:

- *Debrief your recent coaching conversations with another coach.* Strong Coaching Pods provide a relational outlet to talk coaching with a coach. Find a coach to talk to about your coaching. Learn from each other.
- *Ask a coach mentor to listen to you coach.* Don't try this early in a coaching relationship. Establish trust first. The planter you coach will need to be comfortable with a coach mentor listening. When the planter you are coaching sees how much you care about him, he will trust you more.
- *Record your coaching conversations for your review.* Be clear with the person you coach about the purpose of your recording—you want to improve your coaching. The recording is for your ears only. Invite him to be part of the feedback process as well.
- *Pray before each conversation for God to help you listen well.* Hopefully, you are coaching planters based on God's prompting. If coaching is an act of obedience for you, ask God to help you to obey.

Listening is unnatural—discipline and hard work are required. Use these practices to improve your skills. Listening begins with the work of the Holy Spirit bearing fruit in you. Your coaching will increase in value as you listen.

The Listening Coach

People are drawn to listeners, not talkers. People talk to us twenty-four hours a day—if not in person, then via podcasts, social media, email, etc. But a great coach is a great listener. Great listeners ask insightful questions because they are genuinely curious about another person's story. They also listen for what God is doing in the heart of the storyteller.

Check the statements that best describe your coaching.

	The Practices of the Listening Coach
	I coach in a listening environment free from distractions.
	I summarize back what I hear planters saying.
	I ask follow-up questions based on the previous answers.
	I take notes during my coaching conversations.
	I talk no more than 20 percent of the time.

Be Coached . . .

1. What *could* you do to grow in this quality?

2. What *will* you do to grow in this quality over the next thirty days?

3. Who could help you?

My Coach Helps . . .

My coach helps me to feel that I am not alone at the ministry. Besides that, being coached helps me to get the perspective of life, marriage, families, and ministries of others that increase my knowledge and attitude regarding specific situations. Coaching is a great instrument in my toolbox that's helping me think about my future ministry, take care of young pastors and church planters and give them different points of view in a friendship environment.

Fabian Perea
Calvary En Español Church
Englewood, Colorado
www.englewood.thecalvary.org

 **CHAPTER 8**

The Cheering Coach

My first trip to Canada was extraordinary. I fell in love with the beauty of the country and her people. If you have ever been to Calgary and ventured to Lake Victoria, Lake Louise, or Banff in the Canadian Rockies, you can relate to my awe. The Canadian Rockies and the surrounding area loudly declare the glory of God.

Our mission team from South Carolina was in Calgary to help Southwinds Church prepare for their first Sunday. Months of preparation by the local core team and Taylors First Baptist Church was complete. One of our assignments was door-to-door invites in neighborhoods close to the new church. The first time I ever went cold calling for Jesus was as a nine-year-old, so this was not new to me; but learning about Canadians was. What did they value? How could I turn a cold call into a warm call?

"Talk about your admiration of Canada's beauty," local leaders advised. As I walked down the streets of a clean suburban neighborhood, against the incredible backdrop of the Canadian Rockies, admiration was easy. But blank stares met my best efforts to sell my admiration.

Maybe it was the group of construction workers I approached that inspired my next step, or God, or both. I had discovered in the morning newspaper that their National Hockey League team, the Calgary Flames, was kicking off its season in less than a week. "What do you think about the Flames this year?" I asked. The blank stares turned into passion and great conversations. The cold turned to warm, and I had a new way to start great conversations for the rest of the trip.

Canadians use an awkward word to describe their passion for their team, at least for someone from the U.S. "Who do you cheer for?" they asked. Cheering explains what happens on the sidelines of college football games—at least to me.

Weird, overcommitted zealots cheer and scream into megaphones. I prefer our common term in the U.S., "fanatic," to describe my zeal for the New Orleans Saints and the Tennessee Volunteers.

Cheering Is Awkward

The word *fanatic* evolved from an English word that meant "furious." Winston Churchill said, "A fanatic is someone who can't change his mind and won't change the subject."[1] The word sounds like what the Canadians mean when they say cheering—or worse.

Most of us cheer for something or someone—and we are not ashamed to do so. How about you? I love watching my grandsons play football. One of my daughters rides horses; another daughter is in theater; and my third daughter works for a software company, is a wife, and a mother. I never hold back my loudest cheers for those closest to me, nor do I wonder what anyone thinks about my enthusiasm. Football, hunting, exercise, children, grandchildren, or Facebook may bring out your wildest cheerleading side.

A New Baby Has Arrived

Learning to redirect our cheering voice is crucial for coaches. Of all the voices church planters hear, the cheering voice is the one that tends to disappear.

New churches are like new babies. When a new baby arrives, the crowds cheer loudly. Everybody wants to see, touch, and hold them. People you barely know come bearing gifts. Parties are held in honor of your new bundle of joy, and babysitting is offered for free. People offer to be surrogate grandparents, aunts, and uncles, and meals are delivered to your front door.

But the fanfare stops the moment someone's newer baby arrives. Reality sets in with sleepless nights, trips to the doctor, temper tantrums, and financial pressure. As the raving fans disappear, on some lonely nights you may question whether the timing was right for this new baby.

Sadly, this can happen with new churches. The cheering crowds, gifts, special services, and prayers are usually a part of the early days of a new church. And yet there's something healthy about moving on from this stage. You don't want to be a baby church forever. That is not why babies are born.

A Church Planter's Biggest Fan

Barnabas is a hero to us coach-types. His nickname meant "son of encouragement" and was inspired by his character and behavior (Acts 4:36). He was generous, loyal, and encouraging. And the people around him noticed. A church planter needs a safe relationship with a Barnabas coach who cheers for him. He needs someone he trusts to honestly and appropriately process the criticisms, warnings, and advice he receives.

> A church planter needs a safe relationship with a Barnabas coach who cheers for him.

All cheerleaders are not created equal. For some, encouragement is a spiritual gift—and they use their gift well. But every coach should cheer. *Why don't we cheer more often?*

1. We don't know what to cheer about.
2. We feel like it's inauthentic.
3. We don't think it is needed or wanted.
4. We are disappointed in the person we are coaching.
5. We feel we are manipulating through cheering.
6. We have never had a cheering coach, so we don't know how one looks.

Why don't you cheer more often? Was it left off the list? Rather than handle the objections one at a time, here is one filter that will answer most objections. Replace your church planter's name (or someone else you are coaching) with the name of your favorite sports team. See if you can use the same excuses to stop cheering for your team—not likely. Then answer this question:

*What steps will I take to cheer for leaders
around me in the next thirty days?*

Coaching legend John Wooden told a story about cheering. Wooden taught his players to affirm a teammate who helped them score a basket. One player asked what to do if the teammate that helped them was not looking. Wooden answered, "He will always be looking."[2]

The church planter you coach will "always be looking" for encouraging words. I heard someone say, "The glass is always full; sometimes part of it is air, but it is always full." That is the kind of coach I want to be. How about you?

On your quest to advance as a Cheering Coach, consider the following five practices.

Five Practices of the Cheering Coach

Practice 1: I use social media to cheer for the people I coach.

Twitter, Facebook, and Instagram are common platforms for social gatherings via the Internet. Many conversations surrounding social media are negative. But there are positive ways to communicate through these tools.

At the beginning of your planter coaching relationship, ask about all of the social media platforms he uses. Be sure you friend, follow, etc., as soon as possible. Ask to be included on any distribution lists for newsletters or reports. By doing this, with a minimal investment of time, you will be able to hear all the news sent out and celebrate with the church planter. You will be able to pray with insight and send text reminders before and after big days. Here is what to watch for on social media:

Family Matters: Getting to know the family members by name and praying for them builds community. Most planters communicate their daily lives through social media. Investing a few extra minutes on Facebook, Twitter, or Instagram will keep you up-to-date on birthdays, special accomplishments, and Little League baseball scores.

Awesome Ideas: Innovative and strategic thinking is important to leaders. A sign of a leadership rut is that everything stays the same. Remind the planter of his best ideas, and watch for new ideas that will help you lead too.

Great Stories: Nothing is more influential for the gospel than seeing a new church live what they value. Affirm what you see. For example, "I see that you gave a laptop computer to a new church planter near you. The kingdom is important to you. There are plenty of things you could have done for your church with that money. You made a great choice."

Sharp Insights: Twitter is a platform to promote blogs, quotes, stats, and events. Watch for blog posts written by your planter. Read and comment on the blog site or talk about these posts when you connect.

Use a Key Stroke: Spending hours on social media is not a good way of managing your time. However, being strategic and intentional about the time you spend will encourage your planter. Pushing a few buttons on your keyboard will communicate volumes to people around you. Remember, push the buttons!

Facebook	Like, Comment, Share
Twitter	Retweet, Reply, Like
Instagram	Like, Comment, Send

Practice 2: I affirm the activity of God in the planter's life and ministry.

God moves beyond the best efforts of new churches and their leadership. These "God moments" give the planter and his leaders hope. And for the time, they can rest in the truth that results are in God's hands, not theirs. Celebrate what God is doing.

The Cheering Coach goes beyond what is expected to enter into the world of the planters he coaches. The results are greater trust and confidence in you. You get extra points on the "Cheering Test" if you can visit the church for a regular service.

> Your role as cheering coach is not to evaluate, but to celebrate.

Pull out your phone, tablet, or an old-fashioned piece of paper and look for everything you see right about what you experience. Buy your church planter a great lunch the next week and let him know what you sensed God doing and what he does well. Your role as cheering coach is not to evaluate, but to celebrate.

Practice 3: I visit the websites of the planters I coach.

As with social media, a short visit to the website of the planter you coach is a good investment. Become fluent in church details and look for reasons to cheer. Websites provide more details about the church than most social media outlets. Social media provides up-to-the-minute information. A website helps you see the church from different angles. Here are some things to watch for:

Clear Vision: Vision is more than a sermon series and a fancy slogan. Vision is demonstrated by the decisions a church makes. Watch for ways the vision is being lived out and reinforced. Affirm your planter when you see him cast and live the vision.

Active Values: Nothing is more influential for the gospel than seeing a new church demonstrate their values through behavior. Whether it is small groups going to a homeless shelter to serve or the church giving a church planter a laptop, they practice generosity and service. Look for opportunities to celebrate.

Evidence of Growth: New venues and services are encouraging signs that people are being reached. Often, those are challenging times as well. Make sure your planter does not get lost in the painstaking challenges of "new" and miss what God is doing. Celebrate baptism services, small groups, and new staff members.

A New Sermon Series: Church planters work hard to give their people creative, fresh, and relevant messages. Comment, ask questions, and affirm their direction as communicators. And listen to an occasional sermon podcast—you will understand him and his church more afterward.

John Maxwell gives three important questions people have about their leaders. These are questions planters will have for their coaches:

- Can you help me?
- Do you care for me?
- Can I trust you?[3]

Master church details and priorities. Having a grasp on the planter's world will help you become a better coach. When he talks about a leader by name, you make a connection. When he speaks about his sermon series, you have already been listening.

Practice 4: I affirm strengths, gifts, and experiences.

Here are five questions the Cheering Coach answers for the planters they coach:

1. What is the planter doing well? *(Planter's Need: Affirmation).* Decision making is one of the most important functions of a leader. A coach holds up a mirror to the planter, cheering him along for his good decisions and healthy leadership. Although planters may be slow to admit this, they need to hear an answer to the question, "How am I doing?"

2. What examples of gifts, strengths, and character do you see? *(Planter's Need: Encouragement).* A coach shouldn't assume that a planter knows or embraces how God has uniquely wired him. A great place to start is discussing the planter's assessment report and corresponding developmental plan. But more important, a coach must watch for specific examples of gifts, strengths, and character and be quick to affirm them.

Gallup's *StrengthsFinder Assessment* by Tom Rath is a great discussion starter. Buy your planter a copy of the book and discuss the results. PLACE (www.placeministries.org) is an inexpensive online assessment tool that reveals personality, spiritual gifts, abilities, passions, and experiences. If the planter you coach has experienced a formal assessment process, he likely has results like these already; just ask.

3. Where does he struggle the most? *(Planter's Need: Self-Awareness).* Self-awareness describes our view of ourselves (skills, maturity, strengths, etc.). The best way to address a planter's need to grow is to ask questions like, "What is your biggest struggle?" and "Where do you need to grow?" A coach sees blind spots that can affect life and ministry. Periodically a coach needs to say what he sees and coach the planter through a developmental plan.

4. What apparent contradictions do you see? *(Planter's Need: Awareness).* Awareness describes our view of other people and how our actions positively or negatively affect them; awareness is part of emotional intelligence. Our best intentions may not translate well. The way we communicate, lead, and use our influence can be dangerous or self-defeating. A coach provides an early warning system to help a planter discover the shortcomings of his leadership.

5. What are examples of God at work? *(Planter's Need: Faith).* Leaders are pathologically disappointed. Disciples are never made fast enough, the church never grows large enough, and the community is never engaged enough. A coach watches for the work of the Holy Spirit and helps fuel a planter's faith by providing clear examples the planter may have missed. Don't let them overlook the ways God is using them even through routine events and church activities.

Church planter coaches, the planter you coach needs encouragement and your honest feedback. Know and embrace your role in sending well. Here are three steps:

1. Review these five questions with your planter in mind.
2. Use your initial observations to shape your prayers for your planter.
3. Look for opportunities to give them feedback.

Practice 5: I celebrate completed goals and accomplished action steps.

Great coaches take great notes. We want to make the coaching relationship one ongoing conversation. A planter's accountability and accomplishments increase as a result. As these accomplishments increase, great coaches can come alongside church planters and help them celebrate wins, no matter how small.

The biblical principle is as follows: "Iron sharpens iron, and one man sharpens another" (Prov. 27:17). Iron was advanced technology for the original readers of that proverb. Advanced tools of war and work were now possible. Iron was the biblical equivalent of Apple computers and iPhones for us. Sharpening iron added even greater value and productivity to advanced technology.

God will use you as an instrument to sharpen your planter, and you will be sharpened as well. Review his goals and actions and help him reevaluate their relevance. Give him the opportunity to change, revise, or recommit to them. Give a loud cheer for every accomplished goal or action.

> As these accomplishments increase, great coaches can come alongside church planters and help them celebrate wins, no matter how small.

Check the statements that best describe your coaching.

	The Practices of the Cheering Coach
	I use social media to cheer for the planters I coach.
	I affirm the activity of God in the planter's life and ministry.
	I visit the websites of the planters I coach.
	I affirm strengths, gifts, and experiences.
	I celebrate completed goals and accomplished action steps.

The Cheering Coach

Barnabas was nicknamed the "son of encouragement." He took John Mark on a mission trip even when Paul thought it was a bad decision. Great coaches can come alongside church planters and help them celebrate wins, no matter how small. They can also help church planters get out of demoralizing ruts in life and ministry and move forward again.

Be Coached . . .

1. What *could* you do to grow in this quality?

2. What *will* you do to grow in this quality?

3. Who could help you?

My Coach Helps . . .

My coach helps me to think through tough decisions. He helps to draw the answers to questions out of me rather than answering them for me. He encourages me and, more important, pushes me to Christ as he listens and asks quality questions. My coach helps me to think through things rather than depending on others for answers.

Adam Sewell
The Well Church
Pittsburgh, Pennsylvania
www.thewellpgh.org

 **CHAPTER 9**

The Praying Coach

Heather Bond talks vividly about falling in love with her husband, Matthew, and his passion for God, people, and church planting. The Bonds moved from Fort Worth, Texas, to Vancouver Island, British Columbia, to plant Ekklesia Community Church (www. ekklesiabc.ca) in Sidney, British Columbia. Her excitement is evident in words she uses to describe their church planting dreams:

> Oh, the adventure I saw in this man and in our future! We stepped into the water of faith, and the rushing river of God's plan led us to planting a church three thousand miles from home, in a land where we knew no one but God. And you know what? I love this adventure our faithful God has us on!

Heather is also honest about the challenges of planting. She says, "A church planter's passion can lead to always being on the go, always doing more—a never-resting kind of lifestyle. And the dreams can become quite scary when you feel ill-equipped, overworked, and lonely."

Heather was trained as a coach through the Send Network at the same time as her husband, Matthew. She learned how God could use coaching and soon experienced it as well. Heather wrote,

> Coaching is a lifeline for my husband as a church planter— and it's a lifeline for our marriage, too. Coaching draws my husband back to God's plan, power, and ability to

accomplish His will through him. It helps him fight the spiritual battle of low self-esteem and low productivity by focusing his attention on what God wants him to do next.

Heather writes about how coaching helps planters dream, hear from God, believe in themselves, and unwind. She also describes how coaching spurs planters from visions of grandeur to real-life success: "By defining success, creating action plans, and being held accountable, my church planter can accomplish God's plans and experience the joy of every victory."[1]

Don't Forget

Matthew and Heather's story recounts the adventure and the reality of church planting. Part of our role as coaches is to remind church planters of their humanity. A church planter is a person, not a project or a worker on the kingdom assembly line.

Planters enter the picture with a strong vision and bold faith that God is going to plant His church. Although self-doubt may be in their secret thoughts, nothing about them suggests that. Wayne Cordeiro reminds leaders:

> We don't forget we are Christians. We forget that we are human, and that one oversight alone can debilitate the potential of our future.[2]

Prayer reminds us that we are human. And the Spirit intercedes: "Likewise the Spirit helps us in our weakness . . ." (Rom. 8:26). Great coaches are prayer warriors and prayer catalysts.

Ready, Set, Go

A robust assessment process has helped a planter and his planting wife gain the endorsement of an experienced assessment team. Vision, communication skills, and past behavior are considered. Marriage, spiritual health, and emotional health also are parts of the process. Developmental suggestions accompanied the coveted green light to plant.

The process affirms the strengths and potential of a planting couple. Their personal approval rating has never been higher. A sending church has expressed great confidence and is heavily invested in the success of the plant. Other financial partners, including the denomination, are all on board. In the middle of all the fanfare, we can all forget the planter is human.

Planting families face temptation, just as Jesus faced temptation. Planters' wives struggle with identity and the desire for security. Self-doubt, frustration, and isolation are the planter's enemies. Spiritual warfare intensifies as his commitment to push back lostness increases.

The positive fanfare helps a planting couple establish early momentum. The coach enters a relationship as one who will help maintain momentum—and pray as the couple comes face-to-face with their humanity.

Champion of the Soul

A coach provides sacred space for the planter to be real. He is a champion of the planter's soul and the fruitfulness of his plant. The coaching relationship provides one line of defense against the planter losing himself. He is a disciple of Jesus first. All other roles, responsibilities, and assignments flow from his relationship with Jesus.

> A coach provides sacred space for the planter to be real.

I was driving from Ohio to West Virginia in the late nineties when I received a memorable phone call. My good friend Mike was launching a new church in Cincinnati that Sunday. His report was electric. God had done a good work through Mike, Jennifer, and the planting team. Over three hundred people attended on launch day. I distinctly remember experiencing an adrenaline rush as I heard the story, thinking, *God is going to do this!*

We live for those stories, yet our system must have champions, not just of stories, but of the *souls* of the planters and their families.

Coaches, planter care teams, trainers, and catalysts must all be champions of the soul. But in this system, the planter coach bears a significant portion of the responsibility. Great coaches are spiritually aware. They love success stories of life change, community impact, and healthy congregations. But intercessory prayer is a high value and practice. Great coaches know planters are people; they are followers of Jesus. They are also aware the battle is not merely strategic or tactical, but is spiritual warfare.

Seek God for the City is a forty-day prayer emphasis that helps people pray for their cities. One day focuses on praying for pastors and church leaders:

> Pray that pastors and church leaders will be filled with wisdom; that they will be honored by those they serve; that God will pour His spirit upon them in power and humility; giving fresh intimacy with Jesus; for protection from the plots of the evil one against their family; that deep friendships with other pastors will grow.[3]

This prayer captures the challenges pastors face and helps prayer warriors see an example of how to pray accordingly. I first read this prayer years ago, and it has helped shape my prayers for pastors since. Great coaches are prayer warriors and prayer catalysts—they keep the focus on God's ability and the planting couple's humanity.

Jesus the Intercessor

Spiritually aware coaches pray for practical, daily needs in a planter's life. Everything from needing a church meeting place to a child's broken arm is a legitimate prayer concern.

Praying Scripture can add another level of intercession. Jesus taught His disciples how to pray through a prayer famously known as the Lord's Prayer (Matt. 6:9–15). He provided a template of *how* to pray, but watching Jesus pray gives an example of *what* to pray.

Praying what Jesus prayed on behalf of our planters is living out the values of Jesus. And the most amazing value of Jesus was the visionary, future-focused nature of His praying.

Watch Him pray for us:

"I am praying not only for these disciples but also for all who will ever believe in me through their message. I pray that they will all be one, just as you and I are one—as you are in me, Father, and I am in you. And may they be in us so that the world will believe you sent me." (John 17:20–21 NLT)

To pray beyond the urgent needs of the day is visionary praying. How far did Jesus see into the future when He prayed? He saw up to the moment that you are reading this sentence (and beyond). Jesus prayed for you and the believers around you.

Our view of movement is confined to what we have seen: social, political, and, at times, spiritual movements. Our hearts long for God to do more of what we are already seeing. But God can do more than we can imagine. We see a glimpse of what "more" might look in John 17.

Praying the visionary prayers of Jesus includes praying:

1. Glorify your Son (v. 1).
2. Protect and unite current disciples (v. 11).
3. Keep disciples safe from the evil one (v. 15).
4. Make disciples holy by your truth (v. 17).
5. For the unity of future believers (v. 21).

Spiritually aware coaches pray with planters. Praying like Jesus said to pray is important. But praying like Jesus prayed takes prayer deeper.

On your quest to advance as a Praying Coach consider the following five practices:

Five Practices of the Praying Coach

Practice 1: I pray with and for planters I coach.

Every time you pray with a planter, you remind him of his humanity and God's sufficiency. What does it mean to pray *for* someone?

Increased Prayer Coverage. One planter can only pray a limited amount of time each day. For more time invested praying about his dreams, obstacles, and challenges, others need to pray *for* him. The same is true for his wife, his children, and his church. Leaders go through seasons when prayer is particularly challenging. Others can pray instead of him as well as in addition to him.

Respect for heart issues that will derail God's vision. Any leader who thinks he has no character issues reveals a serious character issue. A leader who does not acknowledge moral temptation or spiritual immaturity is spiritually immature. Paul Tripp wrote, "The greatest danger in my life exists inside of me and not outside of me."[4]

Turning my heart toward God. My heart is turned toward something or someone. When I pray, my heart turns toward God. As a coach, this reminds me that I am not the solution. I support; I don't fix—God does. I am merely a servant assigned to wash the feet of another servant for a season of ministry.

Remembering that without Jesus, there is no real fruitfulness. Peter Scazzero warns: "Jesus doesn't say you cannot do things without him. You can plant your church without Jesus." But, he concluded, "The church will produce no lasting fruit."[5] Well-intentioned leaders, church planters included, in the midst of overwhelming pressure move forward quickly, without Jesus.

Reminding us that we are not alone. What would you attempt to do if you knew beyond any doubt that God was with you? Most of us could pass the theology test, but are we aware of His presence on a practical level? What difference would that make? Planters struggle with seasons of feeling isolated. Sadly, these seasons will increase based on how helpless they feel. Prayer reminds planters they are not alone.

Practice 2: I ask planters to pray for me and include specific requests.

Building trust is crucial to any coaching relationship. The peer relationship between the coach and the planter is a platform to build trust. Not only does the vulnerability of the coach lead to greater trust, but the relationship evolves into win-win.

> Building trust is crucial to any coaching relationship.

Coaching involves two disciples in a gospel partnership. The coach leaning on the planter for encouragement and prayer builds trust. Each coaching conversation in our coaching guides ends with the coaching question: How can we pray for each other?

When the coach self-discloses to the planter, the planter receives permission to do the same. When a coach draws life from the planter he coaches, new scenarios emerge. The value of coaching is two disciples in community. Authentic community provides strength. Solomon illustrated the principle with a "triple-braided cord."

A person standing alone can be attacked and defeated, but two can stand back-to-back and conquer. Three are even better, for a triple-braided cord is not easily broken. (Eccles. 4:12 NLT)

Practice 3: I help planters recognize the Holy Spirit's work in their lives.

None of us would purposely forget or ignore God. But leaders move quickly and can accidentally leave God out of the process. Here are questions to prompt planters you coach toward the Holy Spirit's activity:

- What does the Father think about what you are planning?
- What is the Holy Spirit teaching you?

- How is the Holy Spirit convicting you?
- What do you need the Holy Spirit to help you remember?
- How are you helping people hear and obey the promptings of the Holy Spirit?
- Where do you need to experience the power of the resurrected Jesus personally?

In the context of a trusting relationship, these questions are gifts from God. But guard against overusing them, which could render them less effective.

Practice #4: I reference Scripture when coaching.

Sharing Scripture to comfort, encourage, and inform a planter opens hearts to the Holy Spirit's work. Scripture in coaching can become too routine or predictable if overused. Listen for key words from normal conversations like:

- I am *afraid* . . .
- I am *worried* . . .
- I am *stressed* . . .
- I am *unsure* . . .
- I don't have any *peace* . . .

Example: "When you said, 'I don't have any peace,' a Scripture came to my mind: 'You keep him in perfect peace whose mind is stayed on you, because he trusts in you' (Isa. 26:3). Could we stop and pray for a moment? I want to pray that God would help you stay focused on Him and completely trust Him during these tough times."

The tone is encouragement, not rebuke. You are moving the planter back to words of life. The prayer can be short, but meaningful. Then, continue the coaching conversation. How refreshing to take a five-minute Sabbath from the work to pray and hear from God! A new perspective will follow the remaining time together.

The Praying Coach coaches from Scripture content. Here are key questions that take the planter back to the Bible for wisdom from God.

- How does Scripture address this challenge?
- What Scripture has God used during times like these in your past?
- How could the Bible inform this decision?
- In what story from the Bible did leaders face a similar situation?

You are not necessarily looking for a Bible study time, but you are hungry for what God wants. Use a short passage of Scripture or verse with questions like these:

- What specific truth from the passage provides a hopeful perspective?
- How can you turn this truth into action?
- How can you change this passage into a prayer?
- Who else might be encouraged by this passage?

Start your next coaching conversation with an encouraging verse and a prayer. You will remind your planter of God's presence and allow God extra space to work.

Practice 5: I prompt planters to cultivate intercessory prayer teams.

Reminding planters to have an active intercessory prayer team is to remind them they are human. Go deeper about topics vital to the planter and his plant. The cultivation of prayer teams reinforces prayer as an actual value, not merely an aspired value.

As with the prayer relationship between the coach and the planter, the prayer team extends the prayer coverage. Planters and their families are part of a team to push back darkness in a city. Satan's platform in a city remains strong as long as he can keep lost people lost.

The spiritually aware coach will keep the planter accountable for cultivating his prayer team by asking great questions like:

- What is the profile of a prayer team member?
- How is your recruitment going?
- What members need to be added or removed?
- How are you communicating with them?
- What are they learning from you about the discipline of prayer?
- What can you learn from the prayer newsletters of other planters?
- What steps can you take to engage your prayer team on a deeper level?
- How can you show appreciation for their prayer support?

"For though we walk in the flesh, we are not waging war according to the flesh" (2 Cor. 10:3). A Praying Coach is a prayer warrior and prayer catalyst. He understands the nature of the battle. A planter benefits by having a coach who is a valued intercessor.

The Praying Coach

Great coaches invite God into the process of the coaching relationship, praying with and for the person they coach. Great coaches also understand that the only long-term wins in life and ministry come from God's work in the heart.

Check the statements that best describe your coaching.

	The Practices of the Praying Coach
	I pray with and for planters I coach.
	I ask planters to pray for me, including specific requests.
	I help planters recognize the Holy Spirit's work in their lives.
	I reference Scripture when coaching.
	I prompt planters to cultivate intercessory prayer teams.

Be Coached . . .

1. What *could* you do to grow in this quality?

2. What *will* you do to grow in this quality?

3. Who could help you?

My Coach Helps . . .

My coach helps me clarify priorities and helps me think through the process. He offers me mentoring as appropriate, but doesn't neglect being the coach. My coach provides encouragement. It is helpful to have someone that is competent and who cares. He provides me with a neutral perspective on the issues I face. My coach doesn't solve my problems, but helps me see the direction I need to go in.

Ken Cordray
Living Faith Community Church
Coraopolis, Pennsylvania
www.livingfaithcommunitychurch.net

 **CHAPTER 10**

The Pressing Coach

My friend Charlie was a deacon at First Baptist Church in Marrero, Louisiana. For twelve years, I was his pastor. A machinist by trade, Charlie was a big, strong man. Nothing was too difficult for him to repair—from our aging building on Seventh Street to my 1984 silver Nissan Sentra.

Charlie was so determined to care for people that he carried a spotlight in his old, beat-up blue truck to help find their homes at night. You may not have been home or may have pretended not to be home when Charlie came to visit, but that would be on you. He would resort to almost any measure to see you. I never saw anybody love Jesus and care for people quite like Charlie.

My final conversations with Charlie were the best. One week before he died, he saved the best prayer for last. I asked, "Charlie, how are things with your soul?" Charlie said, "Great, how are things with your soul?" He made me answer, and I did, from my heart. Then I prayed for him, and he prayed for me.

Fierce Conversations

Susan Scott wrote in her book, *Fierce Conversations*, "While no single conversation is guaranteed to transform a company, a relationship, or a life, any single conversation can."[1] If we refuse to have fierce conversations with certain people, nobody else will. We have been given unique roles and responsibilities in the lives of people around us.

Some of them are like me—they will not listen to "just" anybody.

Another conversation occurred with my first coach, Bob Logan, years before Charlie. After a one-year coaching relationship, I invited Bob to "speak into my life." Bob had walked with me as my coach during the most intense period of my life to date.

Bob said, "Dino, there seems to be a lot of drama in every room you enter, and the best I can tell, there's only one constant in each of those rooms—YOU." He didn't fix me that day, but God used Bob to usher in a new era of self-awareness.

Bob had a conversation with me that no one else could. What if he had just said nice things, instead of fierce things? What if my teacher who led me to Christ decided to back off of the claims of the gospel? Your next coaching conversation could be life-altering. Your job is incredibly important.

> *Your next coaching conversation could be life-altering.*

Jeff Christopherson sees the kingdom impact of fierce conversations. In *Kingdom Matrix*, he wrote this: "When the words that I speak are true, no matter how difficult they may be, the Kingdom of God is forcefully advanced."[2]

Sober Up

I need people in my life like Charlie and others to ask me the tough questions, to speak directly to me. My friend and coach Eddie Hancock made this confession: "I think sometimes I like to coach because it keeps me in control of the conversation. Then, I don't have to answer the tough questions." That was way too confessional for me. But the greater the pressure, the more vital it becomes that we have those voices who lovingly ask us, "How are things with your soul?"

Peter wrote a letter to followers of Jesus who had been forced to live in places they did not want to live and who faced intense pressure and persecution. The suffering Christians in the region now known as Turkey who read Peter's divine posts were reminded of the finish line. Peter gave them sobering words, along with some encouraging words. We need both, right? He comforted and challenged at the same time:

> Therefore, preparing your minds for action, and being sober-minded, set your hope fully on the grace that will be brought to you at the revelation of Jesus Christ. (1 Pet. 1:13)

"Prepare your minds for action" was a challenge to live with an eye on the finish line. We might say, "Roll up your sleeves and get to work" or "Stop the pity party; you are going to win in the end."

"Be sober-minded" points to the need for clarity. "Sober-minded" is the opposite of being drunk. Pressure can cause confusion and disorientation. Walking in a straight direction is a challenge.

None of us will likely face the exact pressures of the Jesus-followers Peter addressed. But there will be days when planters will wonder how it could be any

> How are things with your soul?

worse. Steve Ogne and Tim Roehl said, "Coaches ask the questions that no one else is asking."[3] The Pressing Coach respects the challenges a planter faces but knows that his role is to keep him focused.

Coaches know when tough conversations and questions are needed. The Pressing Coach is not afraid to have those redemptive conversations. A coach that is "comfort food" for the planter is not a coach; he is an enabler.

A coach keeps the pulse of the planter. When the planter needs professional help, press him to get help. Be a shepherd. Protect the planter, his family, and the gospel.

On your quest to advance as a Pressing Coach, consider the following five practices:

Five Practices of the Pressing Coach

Practice 1: I help the planters I coach create SMART goals.[4]

Jamie Limato—church planter, coach, and coach developer—illustrates the SMART process by comparing the role of a coach to one of an eye doctor. All of us have experienced the enormous, Darth Vader-looking mask moved over our faces and the exam that follows. The eye doctor places a series of lenses over our eyes and asks us to read letters off a chart on the wall. He asks, "How does this look?" "Clearer?" "Less clear?" "Better?" The goal is clear vision. In the same way, a coach helps a church planter see the future more clearly by asking questions and pressing for action.

Creating a SMART goal is a clarifying process similar to that of an eye doctor. Goals or intentions normally begin in a "fuzzy" or "blurred" state. A great coach will help a church planter by asking questions to give clarity.

S—Specific (What?): What do you need to do?

Press: Help the planter describe what he wants to happen.

Fuzzy: Reach people for Christ.

Clearer: I will have gospel conversations.

M—Measurable (How much?): How will you know you are making progress?

Press: Help the planter create tangible markers of success through the process leading to the ultimate numerical goal.

Fuzzy: I will have gospel conversations.

Clearer: I will have ten gospel conversations with ten people.

A—Attainable (What?): What resources do you need to reach this goal?

Press: Help the planter determine the necessary and available people, materials, and time to reach the goal.

Fuzzy: I will have ten gospel conversations with ten people.

Clearer: I will have ten gospel conversations with ten people <u>by investing four hours weekly at Bill's Coffee Shop</u>.

R—Relevant (Why?): Why is this goal important now?

Press: Help the planter determine whether this goal currently merits the time, energy, and people needed.

Fuzzy: I will have ten gospel conversations with ten people by investing four hours weekly at Bill's Coffee Shop.

Clearer: <u>To reach people for Christ</u>, I will have ten gospel conversations with ten people by investing four hours weekly at Bill's Coffee Shop.

T—Time-Specific (When?): When will I complete this goal?

Press: Help the planter create a time frame to focus on the goal.

Fuzzy: To reach people for Christ, I will have ten gospel conversations with ten people by investing four hours weekly at Bill's Coffee Shop.

Clearer: To reach people for Christ, I will have ten gospel conversations with ten people by investing four hours weekly <u>over the next thirty days</u> at Bill's Coffee Shop.

An example of SMART Goals and Actions: *To reach people for Christ, I will have ten gospel conversations with ten people by investing four hours weekly at Bill's Coffee Shop over the next thirty days.*

Action: Enlist three people who will pray for me daily, beginning this week.

Action: Schedule the four hours in two-hour blocks each week over the next thirty days.

Action: Journal my conversations on my phone to monitor important data learned in each conversation.

Action: Spend fifteen minutes each day praying through my journal notes.

Making a goal "smarter" will be an ongoing process of evaluation. The Pressing Coach will ask deeper questions to help the planter:

- Define "gospel conversation."
- Clarify how a successful gospel conversation looks.
- Add and evaluate action items in ongoing conversations.
- Determine how long the conversations may take.
- Make needed adjustments during implementation.

Practice 2: I ask the people I coach to calendar deadlines for their action items.

Imagine being a short-order cook at a restaurant on a busy Friday night. To look at tables filled with hungry people waiting for their food is discouraging. To focus on the sheer volume of orders and myriad of details can be self-defeating. But to focus on the next steps to complete those meals and feed the hungry masses is taking action.

Vision drives the big picture, but action makes vision happen. My first coach, Bob Logan, would stop a coaching conversation, ask me to open my calendar, and schedule a deadline for an action item. Then I would move backward from that date to block the time needed to complete the task by the deadline. He was helping an overwhelmed leader focus on the next steps as opposed to the big picture.

The Pressing Coach is persistent with the "When?" question. He is patient to see that the action is on the calendar. Bob was pressing in a way I needed to be pressed. His tone was never rude or condescending—in fact, just the opposite. Bob was also developing a coach in me as I watched him. As I began to coach, I was comfortable imitating his approach. I learned the value of asking the calendaring questions and saw a coach comfortable pressing for the dates.

Practice 3: I send coaching guides in advance of coaching conversations.

A coaching guide is a series of questions that provides an agenda for coaches and planters to follow. Numerous examples are found in *Sending Well*. These guides will help you stay on task and accomplish more in each conversation.

One of the most powerful coaching exercises I have ever experienced was at a coaching workshop led by Keith Webb with my Send Network coaching colleagues. We were divided into groups of six to eight people and given specific questions to ask someone in the middle of a circle.

When it was my turn in the middle, I chose a topic that was real to me about being a parent. My friends began to question me. All of the questions were open-ended and not necessarily confrontational, but they were highly scripted from different perspectives to help me work through my challenge.

> *God can use great questions to help open the hearts of those you coach.*

The outcome was surprising. God stirred my heart as I answered each question. People who loved me read scripted questions off a page, and as the process continued I began to cry. God's timing was perfect, and I was moved. God can use great questions to help open the hearts of those you coach.

Using coaching guides adds value to a coaching conversation. A coaching guide:

- Starts the coaching conversation in advance.
- Adds intentionality to every meeting.
- Provides a template for new coaches to follow.
- Keeps experienced coaches on track.
- Gives the coach an opportunity to prepare well.
- Reminds the coach and the planter about the meeting.

Here are two final tips to help use the guides well. First, be sure you ask good follow-up questions. Beginning coaches often see guide questions as the only ones they need to ask. Questions in the guide are discussion starters. When you get answers back, write follow-up questions based on their initial answers.

Second, send the guides at least forty-eight hours before the conversation. The planter is reminded of the meeting and is given a fair amount of time to get them back to you. Put a calendar prompt on your phone or computer to remind you to send the questions.

Practice 4: I expect coaching guides to be completed and returned in advance of coaching.

The Pressing Coach knows the importance of keeping the planter accountable. Part of being accountable is being 100-percent committed to the coaching process. When you are coaching with a group of coaches in a region, the way you coach a given planter creates either good or bad coaching culture.

One of the reasons I wanted to coach is that I admired the work of great coaches God placed in my life. My coaches were the type of people I wanted to become. Every coach expected something from me. Their expectations were a gift to me. You are doing the planters you coach no favors by refusing to press them for commitment. Be kind and direct. Explain the importance of the coaching guides in your first meeting. Instruct them to give brief answers to each question.

> You are doing the planters you coach no favors by refusing to press them for commitment.

Look for the answers twenty-four hours in advance. Once you get inside twelve hours of the meeting and have no answers, send another email. If you still have no response, a conversation is in order. Explain the importance of preparation. Let them know how the preparation will make their investment of time more valuable and helpful to them.

Practice 5: I ask strong follow-up questions to help planters create action items.

Keith Webb explained how questions help leaders take action:

> Coaching helps coachees to create action steps that will move them forward toward their goal. While each action step is 100 percent up to the coachee to decide, through dialogue, the coach asks clarifying questions regarding what the action step will look like, how it will be done, and realistic timing.[5]

Here is an example of coaching guides based on 1 Peter 1:13:

Gird: Prepare to travel, work, or fight.
- What is your biggest distraction?
- What is most likely to make you stumble?
- What factors are pushing against you?
- How do you need to prepare for the challenge ahead?
- How will prayer be a part of your preparation?

Sober: Prepare for clarity, focus, and movement.
- What is your biggest question?
- Who is currently keeping you accountable?
- In what three areas in your life do you need the most accountability?
- What previous leadership mistakes do you need to guard against?
- What gifts and strengths do you need to build upon?

Grace: Prepare for doubts, accusations, and disappointments.
- What past failure are you struggling to move beyond?
- What is your biggest fear?
- What have you learned from past disappointments that might help you now?

- How will you remain consistent during the ups and downs of church planting?
- What are your keys to having consistent, sweet fellowship with Jesus?

The Pressing Coach

Most of us lose focus under pressure. Whether the pressure is from family struggles, financial issues, or a fear of failing, a coach can help a leader gain clarity and take action. A coach will not only ask the right questions but will also keep the planter he coaches accountable for taking action.

Check the statements that best describe your coaching.

	The Practices of the Pressing Coach
	I help the people I coach create SMART goals.
	I ask the people I coach to calendar deadlines for their action items.
	I send coaching guides in advance of coaching conversations.
	I expect coaching guides to be completed and returned in advance of coaching.
	I ask strong follow-up questions to help planters create action items.

Be Coached . . .

1. What **could** you do to grow in this quality?

2. What **will** you do to grow in this quality?

3. Who could help you?

My Coach Helps . . .

My coach helps me in understanding that I am not the only one who struggles with issues in church planting; in giving me practical steps of how he was able to navigate through tricky waters or things that he learned when they were not navigated well; in praying for each other through circumstances and rejoicing and mourning together. Coaching provides great accountability and direction. It sets a time and a place that you will have to stop, be asked real questions, and share real-life situations that are happening in your church plant.

Benjamin Bolin
Calvary Church
New Prague, Minnesota
www.calvarychurchmn.org

 **CHAPTER 11**

The Supporting Coach

Jamie Limato hit a wall as a church planter. Well into the church planting process with his wife, Jessica, Jamie wanted to quit. He considered coaching as a possible lifeline, but the options he researched were too expensive.

Jamie's journey into coaching started when he attended orientation for new church planter coaches. Jamie said, "I was invited to be a coach, but I needed a coach myself." During orientation, Jamie volunteered to participate in a public coaching demonstration. He picked an urgent coaching objective based on the current conflict in his church. As a result, he realized he was more desperate for coaching than he thought. And he found a coach who volunteered to help.

Jamie entered his new coaching relationship highly motivated and coachable:

> I jumped right in and was willing to listen, engage, and answer any questions my coach threw at me. My coach not only asked questions, but he listened—and extended a hand of friendship throughout the process. Whether it is right or not, much of a man's identity is wrapped up in what he does. Because I was worn out and discouraged, that affected everything, including my marriage and family. My coach helped me identify key areas I wanted to work on, including my family. He helped me process and think through goals and action items to grow in these

areas. I believe my marriage and family are better because of coaching.

Coaching made a difference for Jamie back then, and it's making a difference now. Aletheia Church (www.aletheianorfolk. com) is well established and healthy. Jamie invests time weekly in being coached and coaching other church planters. He recognizes the value of coaching for church planters through his own experience.[1]

One of our system coaching metrics is that the coached becomes the coach. Jamie now helps coaches throughout North America. Imagine a family of supporting coaches committed to helping church planters. What would it look like if every church planter in your area were experiencing what Jamie and the planters in D.C. and Virginia experience? We need more great coaches.

The Supporting Coach Journey

My coaching had expanded outside the circle of people closest to me. I was coaching more paying customers than ever and feeling good about where things were heading. At the end of a series of coaching conversations with a church planter, I asked for feedback. "What are some ways that my coaching has helped you?"

I don't remember his answer, but I will never forget his answer to my next question: "How can I become a better coach?" His honest response surprised and embarrassed me. He explained, "Sometimes you tell stories and give advice that I don't understand and that totally misses what I am talking about."

My talking, storytelling, and advice-giving defaults were deeply ingrained. Here was my shocking revelation:

- I was telling more stories than I thought.
- I was giving more advice than I thought.
- My advice and stories were not as valuable as I thought.
- I talked too much when I coached.
- My coaching was too much about me and too little about him.

Giving tips, formulas, and shortcuts have been a part of the ways I have "helped" people for years. And nothing was more fun than telling a personal story to provide advice, warning, and empathy. But to be a great coach, my approach had to change.

Change Your Default

Great advice has a place in the kingdom. Church planter coaches affirm the other voices in a church planter's life: sending church pastors, experienced church planting leaders, other church planters, trainers, and mentors. But to add another voice as a coach can be redundant and highly frustrating to the planter.

I never needed more training on how to give advice, although this could have helped. As an advice-giver, I made so many assumptions. I have been practicing for years. We are hardwired to give solutions.

Advice is often overvalued, particularly by the coach. Below are questions to test your advice. Advice is overvalued when:

1. **A lack of information is the assumed problem.** What information is missing? What are the biggest questions in the planter's mind? What are the planter's primary sources of information?

2. **All advice is assumed to be good advice.** What makes this advice good? What makes you qualified to give this advice? What does the planter think?

3. **Good advice and timely advice are considered the same.** What is pushing me to give this advice now?

4. **All advice is assumed to work for all people in any situation.** What makes me think this advice is the right advice for this person?

5. **Advice is given for the wrong reasons.** What is the basis for my compulsion to give advice?

God has given planters everything they need to do His will. Do you believe this? And yes, you are part of God's provision. So, take your role seriously. Don't become too parental. Master the practices of the Supporting Coach. Be a supporter, cheerleader, and friend.

Give God Space

One way a Supporting Coach helps a church planter is to get out of the way. Advice can interrupt the sacred process of a church planter going deeper into his soul to discover what God wants to change. A coach is a supporter and facilitator; he is not a repairman.

Coaches help planters process the urgent. How much money needs to be raised this month? What is the next step in core development in the next two weeks? What tasks need to be addressed before launch next month? A coach who patiently and persistently walks with a planter during urgent seasons increases the value of the relationship.

However, great coaches understand there are deeper, more long-term issues God desires to address in the life of the planter. Only God can fix the deeper issues. Paul Tripp confessed, "I must remind myself that the gospel welcomes me out of my hiding. It welcomes me to face my darkest parts with hope."[2]

On your quest to advance as a Supporting Coach, consider the following five practices:

Five Practices of the Supporting Coach

Practice 1: I avoid giving advice.

The coach approach to advice-giving is different. We have given examples of when coaches need to speak directly into a situation to affirm or warn. Direct communication can be helpful. But be patient and self-aware. The less that is given, the more valuable it becomes.

People have pressed me for advice in the coaching context over the years. How do I keep them on the coaching path without ignoring the request? The first way I normally respond is: "Okay, but you go first." Most of the time I never get a turn, and that is the way I want it. However, my turn may be needed.

After the person I coach has exhausted all his ideas, I give my advice. But a question immediately follows: "What are your thoughts about what I said?" I give him full permission to veto my advice. And you know what? The majority of the time, my well-intended brilliance is vetoed.

As a coach I am not offended when someone says, "No, that won't work because . . . " or (most commonly) "I have already tried that." The coaching process is working when this happens. The leader coached now knows he has a safe place to process options and make decisions. He does not feel manipulated into following the advice of a coach. And most important, he can keep considering other options.

Another way I respond to the request for advice is to ask if there is another time we can talk. I do this only in relationships with people I know well. I explain, "This time is for you to process, but I would love to set up another time for us to talk, exchange information, and talk about our experiences." If carefully done, this helps leaders understand coaching better and have a healthier view of their needs.

One of the most effective coaching constructs I use is to ask the person I coach to become his own advisor. When people I coach feel stuck in a situation, they often shut down their problem-solving skills. I will ask: *What if I came to you with this problem? What advice would you give me?* I am amazed how often this shift in perspective provides breakthroughs for the person coached.

Practice 2: I help clarify the planter's desired outcomes for the coaching conversation.

Each coaching conversation begins with connecting and celebrating. You make a relational connection and celebrate the good things God has done since your last meeting. After an adequate amount of time is invested there, the desired outcomes for the day need to be established.

You establish these outcomes by asking questions like:

- What do you want to work on today?

- What challenge, project, or goal would you like to work on in our time together?
- At the end of our time together, what would you like to walk away with?

If you are working from an agenda created in advance, you will have an idea how your planter wants to use his time. But getting more clarity is important. Part of the skill of the coach is to take a big idea and make it small. If the planter you are coaching is attempting to help twenty new people attend a small group in the next sixty days, you need to process questions like:

- What progress are you making?
- What adjustments are needed?
- What would you like to get out of this conversation to help you move forward?

A coaching relationship is a series of conversations designed to help a planter determine and achieve goals. Each conversation builds upon momentum the planter enjoys by implementing well-crafted action steps.

Practice 3: I keep planters focused on their stated goals and outcomes.

Church planters go fast. A Supporting Coach provides space for a planter to decide where he wants to go and helps him move in the right direction. Ed Cerny explains:

> A busy life is not necessarily a focused life. You can be wildly busy, wheels spinning all the time, and getting nowhere. If you leave Atlanta planning to arrive in Miami, and drive 65 miles an hour heading northeast, you're making great time, but you're still going in the wrong direction.[3]

The Supporting Coach keeps notes and continually reviews the direction the planter decided to go. The last thing the coach wants to see is the planter heading fast in the wrong direction.

Review the big-picture goals to help them stay on course often. I review the goals when I send prep questions, during each conversation, and in the follow-up email. Detours, distractions, and unnecessary exits are avoided at all costs. Here are four ways you can help planters keep moving in the right direction:

Be courageous. The planter has a legitimate need to process. But don't compromise the value of coaching to help him feel good about himself. When you sense the talk is not leading anywhere, be direct. Don't waste the planter's time. Redirect through a question like: *What else do you need to do to move your small groups project forward?*

Be curious but not too curious. Curiosity is an asset to a great coach. Curiosity creates great questions. However, there is a risk that you can become curious about insignificant details. We love to hear people's stories, but sometimes that is a liability. Don't become another distraction.

Be flexible and sensitive to the Holy Spirit. One evening I was scheduled to listen to peer coaches. One of the coaches got some frightening news from the doctor about one of her children that day. We kept our scheduled meeting, and the first question the coach asked was:

I know you received some unsettling news today from your doctor. Would you like to keep our planned agenda or go another direction tonight?

That's an awesome example of coaching flexibility! The Holy Spirit may lead you to give the person you coach the option of changing the agenda. Be flexible.

Be clear. Communicate goals and outcomes constantly. Give the planter a chance to change if you sense he is not making progress. Helping your planter make adjustments due to a current crisis or a change of priorities is a way to be a Supporting Coach. Remember, it is not your agenda, but it is his agenda. You help him with what he wants until he decides to change direction.

Practice 4: I help brainstorm multiple options to provide strategic solutions.

A coach helps planters brainstorm possible actions to produce more thoughtful and strategic action. For example, let's say a planter wants to increase involvement in small groups. He may say, "I will make an announcement this Sunday morning at the end of the service to encourage people to sign up for a small group."

> *A coach helps planters brainstorm possible actions to produce more thoughtful and strategic action.*

If you accept his action without more pressing, you are limiting his results to his first impulse. This is an example of coaching, but not great coaching. A better approach begins with a series of questions, like:

- What makes small group attendance important now? Clarify motivation and relevance, and help define his "Why?".
- How many groups do you have? Help identify current realities.
- How many new people would you like to attend? Help set realistic expectations.
- How soon would you like to reach this goal? Create a sense of urgency and focus.

Now you will help your planter create a goal:

Because I want more of our Sunday morning attendees to experience biblical community over the next sixty days, I want twenty new people to try a small group.

Compare this goal above to the initial action:

I will make an announcement this Sunday morning at the end of the service to encourage people to sign up to attend a small group.

A coach helps planters move from random, disconnected ideas and actions to comprehensive plans. The probability of reaching the goal is greater now because it is more than an impulse.

Your planter is now in a position for some important brainstorming by answering this simple question:

What steps will you take to meet your goal?

Here is a simple brainstorming process:

- Be clear about what is going to happen next. "Let's brainstorm ways you can reach this goal."
- Support your planter by listing his ideas as he gives them.
- Keeping asking, "And what else . . . ?"
- Keep repeating his ideas back to him.
- Don't be afraid of silence.
- When you think he is out of ideas, press for one more.
- Review ideas and ask: "What will you do?"

Capture the next idea, coach the specific action details (who, what, when, where), and keep going. You will review and adjust these actions over your next three to four coaching conversations. A great coach helps turn passion into results through brainstorming.

Practice 5: I ask for personal highlights at the end of each coaching conversation.

Ending a conversation strongly is an essential part of coaching. A fruitful conversation can lose influence without a time to help the planter clarify what just happened. You can help your planter capture new learning by asking,

What were your takeaways from our conversation today?

Help the planter do the work. Resist summarizing the highlights for him. A highlight question helps you see the planter's progress and your coaching effectiveness. You are the note-taker, not the engine behind this process.

More than one question can be included when you ask for highlights. A question opens doors. Here are some additional follow-up questions:

- What specifically did you sense God saying today?
- What step of obedience do you need to take?
- What surprised you about today's conversation?
- What is clearer to you now than before we talked today?
- Who else do you need to talk to about today's coaching?

These questions also serve as a quick check-in for coaches. They help you evaluate the effectiveness of the conversation. "How have I helped the planter achieve the objective of this conversation?" "How has this conversation helped the planter implement his stated goals?"

The final responses to a given coaching conversation are another way to add intentionality. Begin your conversations well, and end them well. That's great coaching.

The Supporting Coach

Everything doesn't work everywhere for everybody. This principle certainly applies to life and ministry. Every church planter has a unique kingdom assignment. Variables abound: the location of a new church, the timing of a planting project, and the attributes of the planter (his background, gifts, and experience) are only a few. What works in Vancouver may not work in the Bronx or Miami.

Check the statements that best describe your coaching.

	The Practices of the Supporting Coach
	I avoid giving advice.
	I help clarify the planter's desired outcomes for the conversation.
	I keep planters focused on stated goals and outcomes.
	I help brainstorm multiple options to provide strategic solutions.
	I ask for personal highlights at the end of each coaching conversation.

Be Coached . . .

1. What *could* you do to grow in this quality?

2. What *will* you do to grow in this quality?

3. Who could help you?

My Coach Helps . . .

My coach helps me process the ups and downs of church pastoring/ planting. He encourages me and pushes me. He helps me think through the reasons why we do things and then helps me set concrete goals in order to move forward.

Eric Baldwin
River City Church
Swissvale, Pennsylvania
www.rivercitypgh.com

 **CHAPTER 12**

The Relating Coach

Ed Cerny is a relating coach. He embodies many of the qualities of a great coach and is a coach worthy to watch and imitate.

An influential leader in two church plants in Myrtle Beach, South Carolina, Ed's day job was as Marketing Professor at Coastal Carolina University. He holds a PhD from the University of South Carolina. Coaches' Corner is his coaching brand that gives him a platform to coach business, civic, and church leaders.

Ed loved to coach church planters, but to him it was more than an assignment. Coaching was a fully engaged relationship. Planters were people to Ed. He loved them and their families. Ed connected with them beyond coaching conversations. Some planters stayed connected with Ed for years beyond the coaching relationship. He prayed for them in detail and served them well.

Here is Ed's story:

> What I loved most about coaching planters was meeting planters from all over; it was a delight to work with them all, even those who did not follow through with the assignments.
>
> Planters knew they were safe in discussing issues with me. I helped them by being a sounding board for them. I always said that whatever we said in our conversations stayed between the two of us. All I have is my integrity. Once I compromise my integrity, I have nothing.

I helped them by praying for them and their families. I saw God work. Week by week, we'd pray over issues together, and down the road God would answer in His own way. It was a blessing to see how He answered so many prayers: site location, funding, leadership in the church, family issues, and more.

I knew everyone's family—names, birthdays, and anniversaries. I'd add their prayer requests to my prayer list. I started doing a daily prayer list in 1983. I still have all the sheets (917 sheets to date). I pray over each sheet weekly, for a full year, then it goes into a large book binder. Prayer is important to me because this is the way I can connect with other people.

God used Ed in greater ways than being a church planter coach. When Ed was your coach, you also had a strong intercessor. And when Ed was your coach, you had a lifelong friend.

Church planters need relationships. And yet they live in a vortex of pressure to produce. Danger and spiritual warfare greet the planter who does not have a coach like Ed Cerny in his life.

The Planter You Coach Is Your Brother

The biblical mandate to live in community is clear. Dhati Lewis, Director of BLVD (NAMB) and lead pastor of Blueprint Church in Atlanta, often says,

> The church is not like family; it is family. God is literally our Father, Jesus is literally our elder brother, and we are literally brothers and sisters in Christ.[1]

And I would add that the planter you coach is not "like a brother to you"; he is your brother. To fully understand brotherhood as it applies to coaching or any relationship in the body of Christ, you must start with a literal interpretation.

Our daily dialogue with coaching leaders throughout North America provides plenty of learning. The value of the relationships is a constant topic of conversation. God builds a new depth of community when planters have these types of relationships. And leaders notice a difference. Here are samples of feedback we have received about church planter coaching:

Relationship building has been the most critical and beneficial aspect of the coaching process. Getting to know the coaches as well as the planters beyond just planting has changed the dynamic of coaching. Real people being real with one another always changes the relationship.

God is working through the coaching relationships. The coach and coachee develop biblical community and in turn utilize these skills with other leaders in their respective churches and church plants. Coaching seems to break down barriers ministers often have with one another.

Dependability and faithfulness count more than expertise. Coaching is a ministry of presence and encouragement even as the Holy Spirit challenges presuppositions and practices.

We Don't Coach or Relate Identically

Gary Smalley and John Trent[2] gave us a gift when they chose animals to represent different personality types. Insights abound for coaches as they understand the personality of the planter they coach as well as their own.

Style	Lion (Aggressive)	Beaver (Detailed)	Otter (Lively)	Golden Retriever (Calm)
Strength	Pressing	Planting	Cheering	Serving
Weakness	Impersonal	Impatient	Distracted	Passive
Pace	100-Yard Dash	10K	Half-Marathon	Marathon
Gift	Vision	Intentionality	Encouragement	Consistency
Needs to Improve	Relating	Supporting	Pressing	Cheering

The Lion Coach

The Lion Coach is focused, strong, and task-oriented. As a coach, the Lion brings focus to the relationship. He will help a planter take personal responsibility for what is happening in his plant. The Lion is a visionary who can see above circumstances to what God has planned. He will press a planter for action.

The Lion can be a great coach, but self-awareness is important. Soaring with his strengths of focus and vision is vital. Enjoying the relationship and seeing the planter as his brother is important, too. Appreciating the uniqueness of the planter and his context will be a challenge. The Lion must learn to trust God to use the coach relationship.

The Beaver Coach

The Beaver Coach is a builder and a detailed planner. A process thinker, he will press for plans and actions. When a planter is creating and enhancing systems, a Beaver coach will be fully engaged. He brings intentionality to the table. One of his coaching strengths will be the great coaching quality of planting. During critical early days of planting involving systems design, implementation, and execution, the Beaver coach will be at his best.

He will struggle at times with being patient in the learning process of the planter he coaches. "You're just not doing this right" will be the words the Beaver will struggle to hold back. Although pointing out planter inconsistencies may be a necessary coaching conversation, being patient with the process will make the Beaver a better coach.

The Otter Coach

The Otter Coach is relational, fun, and enthusiastic. If encouragement and affirmation are what a planter needs, an Otter coach will be helpful. He will see the glass as always full and will celebrate the ministry wins.

The Otter Coach's struggle is opposite that of a Lion Coach. A coaching conversation could evolve into a party. Personal goals and ministry outcomes may not receive the focus needed. An Otter Coach needs to focus on pressing for action. Journaling action steps from every conversation will help the Otter maintain focus.

The Golden Retriever Coach

The Golden Retriever Coach is calm, steady, and loyal. When a planter needs a calming influence for his chaotic world, he will appreciate the Golden Retriever Coach. During a crisis, whether it involves church or family, you want this coach. A Golden Retriever Coach will be more pastoral and sympathetic.

The Golden Retriever Coach tends to avoid direct communication with the planter. Pointing out inconsistencies or a planter's disregard of the coaching agreement will be difficult. Cheering may need more focus for the steady Golden Retriever. Looking and praying for opportunities to speak directly is a good next step.

Be Self-Aware

Look in the mirror. Your strengths, personality, gifts, and experiences can push your coaching forward in a positive way to help a church planter. However, they can be a negative force that weakens your coaching. Understanding who you are is a significant step forward in becoming a great coach.

On your quest to advance as a Relating Coach, consider the following five practices.

Five Practices of the Relating Coach

Practice 1: I use notes from previous coaching conversations to help me prepare to coach.

Coaches vary in their practice of using notes. I have coached with and without notes. There are strengths to both approaches. Note-taking aids listening during a coaching conversation. Details are captured in our notes that would be lost if we relied solely on memory. And relating to others is all about details.

Have you ever had a conversation in which a new friend or acquaintance remembered a detail about your life? How did you feel? When a coach remembers details about our lives, we feel that they care about us. And when every conversation with that coach involves them remembering the things that are important to us, the relationship is deepened and strengthened.

We encourage a follow-up email from the coach. This brief email captures major actions and important reminders from the conversation. Follow-up emails capture important notes that can help you prepare for the next conversation.

Practice 2: I begin each coaching conversation by making personal, informal connections.

Planters navigate all kinds of situations daily: people in crisis, financial needs (church and personal), family obligations, engaging the lost in their community. Many of these situations require a huge amount of emotional, mental, and spiritual energy.

Make personal, informal connections with those you coach. This communicates to them that they are not alone, and that they can step outside their "must produce" world for a time to recharge. You can ask:

- What is the best movie you've watched lately?
- What is the best book or article you have read this month?
- What happened lately that made you laugh the hardest?
- How are things going at home?
- What is your family highlight this month?
- What is one of your favorite childhood memories?
- Where is the most unforgettable place you ever visited?

Questions like these are in most of our coaching guides. You can design your questions, but be sure that all of the conversation does not revolve around work or ministry. You will learn as much about the planter you are coaching during "small talk" as you will during church plant talk.

Personalities are different. I am an Otter who loves relationships. I have to guard against losing track of time during the connecting part of the conversation. I love connecting personally with the people I coach. The personal details are easier for me to remember than ministry details. But Otter coaches like myself can lose focus quickly and spend too much time connecting.

One of my past coaches was a Lion Coach. He was great at staying on task and making our meetings productive, but he had to discipline himself to connect. We would talk about running at the beginning of each conversation. He would move on from the topic quickly, however. Connecting was important to him, but productivity was more important. I valued his coaching as well as his self-discipline.

Jeff Christopherson wrote, "God's plan for His Kingdom is not individualistic autonomy. Isolation is inspired from a far darker realm. It is the genius of the Body working interdependently that propels unstoppably the great purposes of the Kingdom."[3] We are charged to relate well to the planters we coach by making personal connections with them.

Practice 3: I begin my coaching meetings on time.

Paul, writing to the Philippians, said, "Let each of you look not only to his own interests, but also to the interests of others" (Phil. 2:4). One very practical way to look out for the interests of the planters we coach is to start our coaching meetings on time.

Starting coaching meetings on time shows respect for the planter and his time and gives him an example to follow as well. Here are some tips that will help:

- Confirm the start time twenty-four hours in advance with the planter you are coaching to avoid any miscommunication and confusion.

- The day of the conversation, set a calendar reminder for twenty minutes before the start time of the conversation. Refuse to "do just one more thing."
- Use the twenty minutes before the start of the coaching conversation to prepare your heart and mind to coach.

Starting meetings on time is important in the business world and can be a sign of a well-run organization; starting on time is equally important in coaching.

Practice 4: I end my coaching meetings on time.

A coach who relates well starts his meetings on time—he also ends them on time. We all have phone calls we dread to make because we know we'll be tied up for what seems like forever. What do we usually do in those situations? We avoid making the call. As coaches, we never want our planters to dread coaching conversations because we don't know how to end them.

A great coaching conversation has an agenda as well as a progression. Our *Coaching Dive* contains these elements:

Connect	What's new?
Celebrate	What's working?
Explore	What's happening?
Capture	What's important?
Act	What's next?

Plenty of coaching agendas exist like the one above. What is important is that you have an agenda. How much time you spend in each element may vary based on the particular conversation. You may choose to time each section or keep focused on the end time and pace yourself differently to get there. But I recommend that you keep the agenda at sixty minutes or less. You will be a better coach if you do. Here are some ways to consistently end your coaching meetings on time:

- Confirm the ending time at the beginning of the coaching conversation.
- Set a timer with a reminder built in for when there are ten minutes left in the meeting time.
- When the timer goes off, let the planter know there are ten minutes left before the end of the meeting.

Ending your coaching conversations on time builds deeper trust and respect with the planters you coach. More energy will be maintained throughout a series of conversations and more will be accomplished.

Practice 5: I discuss a coaching agreement at the beginning of each relationship.

Any new endeavor requires clear parameters in order to be successful. Coaching church planters is no different. Coaching is an intentional relationship, not merely hanging out or troubleshooting.

A coaching agreement sets up the coaching relationship for success. An example of a coaching agreement is in Appendix G. Both sides clarify the commitment and goals. This agreement provides the baseline expectations of a coaching relationship.

If the planter is not keeping basic commitments for fruitful coaching, remind him gently. Keeping appointments, being on time, returning prep questions, and following through with action will make or break coaching. Go back to the agreement when necessary.

You will get important clues about the church planters you coach from your initial discussion of the coaching relationship. Why does he want to be coached? When has he received coaching in the past? How does he envision the coaching relationship unfolding? Set clear expectations.

Coaching is a working relationship. Hard work, patience, and persistence are required from both the coach and the planter. Robert Hargrove concluded: "Coaching is having both the toughness and the compassion to skillfully intervene in people's learning processes."[4]

Coaching is a relationship between two disciples. The Relating Coach understands the planter he coaches is his brother and is aware of how his relational style impacts coaching.

The Relating Coach

Coaching is a relationship, and relationships take time. Coaching involves intentional, one-on-one conversations that require patience, listening, and asking questions. Coaching is more of a process than a discussion about a particular topic. A great coach is comfortable with an ongoing, relational journey toward God's purposes.

Check the statements that best describe your coaching.

	The Practices of the Relating Coach
	I use notes from previous conversations to help me prepare to coach.
	I begin each coaching conversation with personal, informal connections.
	I begin my coaching meetings on time.
	I end my coaching meetings on time.
	I discuss a coaching agreement at the beginning of each relationship.

Be Coached . . .

1. What *could* you do to grow in this quality?

2. What *will* you do to grow in this quality?

3. Who could help you?

My Coach Helps . . .

My coach is for me and is a real blessing. First, it is not often we have time when someone takes care of us. I love the connection with him. I feel appreciated and loved by him; he is human. Second, I have a coach who is humble with great experience in ministry. He asks really good questions to help me explore important parts of my life. The coaching process is necessary for every planter who wants to stay on track.

Benoit Marcoux
Come Jesus Church
Mont-Saint-Hilaire, Quebec Canada
www.com-jesus.com

 **CHAPTER 13**

The Planting Coach

Leo Humphrey was one of my mentors in the eighties. He was an itinerant evangelist and missionary who was passionate about people in Central America. Everybody loved Leo.

Leo carried large rolls of "Jesus" stickers with him everywhere. People of all ages loved getting stickers. He often walked into businesses or met people on the street with a sticker and asked, "Has anyone told you they loved you yet today?" And then he would reply, "I love you, and Jesus loves you—that's two." God taught me so much by watching Leo.

By his confession, Leo had no balance in his life—but not in a bad way. He quit his job to be a full-time, partner-supported missionary and evangelist. Leo told me on more than one occasion, "I've never found the word 'balance' in the Bible."

> *We often wring our hands nervously, seeking to create balance in our lives.*

We often wring our hands nervously, seeking to normalize our existence or create balance in our lives. Lots of good energy is wasted trying to do something that is impossible. Since balance is unlikely, what's worth throwing my life out of balance?

Balanced Coaching

Ron Shepard is the Send City Missionary for Seattle, Washington. Coaching church planters is a vital part of his strategy to help church planters pursue their unique kingdom assignment. He wrote about Seattle coaching:

> Coaching is part of a team approach for how we work with and support church planters. Our experience and research have demonstrated that it normally takes a team to help a planter discover and stay on the path to God's preferred future. For example, our Western mindset says that we deserve pain-free and trouble-free lives. When life deals us the opposite, we may blame or feel sorry for ourselves, while devoting time and energy to coping. This affects our attitudes and can create a pattern to find ways of serving God inside boundaries set by the aims of self-protection.
>
> We help planters face what is normal (frustration, disappointment, sickness, conflict, persecution, danger, and stress) and maintain their focus on Christ and His vision and plan for their lives and work.[1]

Ron's perspective on "what is normal" is invaluable. The early passion that accompanies a planter and his family meets the realities of life. Not only does a planter need help to process the realities, but he also needs help processing the purpose of those realities. Why is this so difficult?

Coaches help planters manage the realities of two worlds:

1. **Planter development, discipleship, and care (the person).** His relationship with God, his wife, and his children involve never-ending habits and responsibilities. Self-leadership and personal growth are corresponding challenges.

2. **Church planting fruitfulness, mission, and growth (the plant).** Efforts to reach people for Christ, make disciples, multiply churches, and become financially viable can be sources of both great joy and frustration.

Pressure comes from all directions. Do I coach the planter? Do I coach the plant? Our default in coach development leans strongly toward coaching the planter. We want our coaches to be out of balance from the beginning. Here are four reasons we focus on the person.

Why We Focus on the Person

1. The planter is made in the image of God. God is well pleased with him before he plants. We want him to walk in the acceptance of the gospel. A deadly performance trap is the alternative.

2. Most planters will not be founding pastors. Founding pastors who plant a church and remain the pastor for their lifetime are rare. No matter the "success" of the plant, the planter will likely move on as a leader. Coaches resist seeing the long-term future and identity of the planter through this one assignment.

3. A planter's family is his first calling. The church planting assignment may change, but his family will be with him for life. Blaming the exceptional pressures from "the ministry" is our default. But no matter my vocational choice, exceptional family pressures meet me. The Planting Coach will press for accountability. Coaching time invested in the family is a lifetime investment.

4. Vocational identity is a male default. Talking about the plant is always early on the relational agenda. Conversations gravitate toward typical "How's your church?" questions. Whatever business might be, we men love to talk business. We tend to see the world through work. The coach offers an out-of-balance relationship in an attempt to counterbalance other relationships.

Seasons of Planting

You can't be 100-percent focused on work and family at the same time. The math doesn't work. So the relentless pursuit of balance is impossible. Some seasons of church planting require more energy going toward the plant; other seasons require more energy toward personal and family matters. Coaches help create awareness of the seasons and coaches accordingly.

Part of a planter's assignment includes his church. The Planting Coach knows this and lets the planter set the agenda. He helps him focus more on the church-intense seasons of planting, such as the pre-launch phase. But the Planting Coach also monitors the seasons and makes the planter aware that a corresponding season of focusing on family is necessary.

The purpose of this chapter is to identify how a church planter coach helps planters plant well. Ed Stetzer and Daniel Im wrote, "Church planting, though profoundly entrepreneurial, is not a solitary effort; church planting must be a partnership."[2] One of the planter's most important partners is his coach.

On your quest to advance as a Planting Coach, consider the following five practices.

Five Practices of the Planting Coach

Practice 1: I ask questions aimed toward specific church planting outcomes.

Church planting metrics are important:

- Planters plant churches to reach people for Christ.
- Planters plant churches to make disciples.
- Planters plant churches that multiply.
- Planters plant churches to glorify God.

Throughout *Sending Well*, we have reviewed a coaching platform that includes the King's message and the King's glory. Tangible results—reaching people, making disciples, multiplying churches, and growing toward financial sustainability—are worth reporting and measuring. We value what we measure.

Measurable results are a relevant coaching topic. We have coaching guides that review metrics. Metrics—or as we not so affectionately call them, "nickels and noses"—do not have to be a negative discussion, particularly with the coach.

Measurement of tangible results should always take context into consideration. A golf score principle would simplify the theological and missiological discussion of measuring results: A golfer should always play against yesterday's score.

In our church planting efforts, we struggle between two polarities. We either measure a planter's results through a launch-large, grow-fast lens, or refuse to measure results at all.

Here is a compromise: Help a planter measure results based on yesterday's results. Competing with the planter in the next town will either destroy or inflate your planter's ego. But in any context, a planter needs to measure progress and keep moving forward.

> Measurement of tangible results should always take context into consideration.

Here is an example of a coaching conversation built on this principle:

1. What progress have you made since our last conversation?
2. What are the highlights of your *monthly report*?
3. What part of the report would you like to improve?
4. What steps can you take to improve this part?
5. What other specific tasks do you need to accomplish before we talk again?
6. What help do you need?
7. How can we pray about these challenges? (Pray specifically for measurable results.)

Church planters continually hear statements like: "Build in the beginning what you want in the end." This is true and necessary for them, but the reality is that this happens in many areas through ongoing choices. This isn't about making one decision, but successive decisions over time. The Planting Coach helps church planters by asking questions aimed at outcomes, yielding the end results they want.

Practice 2: I coach toward development needs that surfaced during the assessment process.

Developmental steps are a part of most effective church planter assessments. Ask your church planter for a copy of his assessment—particularly the developmental suggestions. Coaches add value to an assessment process by staying focused on the growth edges the assessment reveals. Keep the growth conversation alive. Ask questions like:

- What did you learn from your church planter assessment?
- How were you encouraged by the process?
- What areas of personal growth need your primary focus now?

If there was no formal assessment, have a meeting with the planter to discuss a simple growth plan. If possible, add a vested third party to the discussion. This third party could be:

- The sending church pastor
- A church planting leader
- A trusted friend

Three perspectives can inform a relevant development plan. The planter, the coach, and the pastor, leader, or friend all answer the question: "Where does the planter need to grow?" The brainstorming process could produce a daunting list. Part of the process includes the coach using his skills to help the group narrow the list to three-to-five focus areas.

Discovering developmental areas should be the priority. Assessment processes reveal potential as well as competencies. "Potential" is positive if a plan is in place to catalyze growth. Coaching helps a planter identify development issues, prioritize them, and set related goals and actions.

Here are two tips to help you coach toward development issues identified during assessment:

1. Start with strengths. Tony Stoltzfus, on his blog www. coach22.com, asks a great question to help with this: "Take a look at your strengths. All strengths tend to have corresponding weaknesses. What are yours?" He goes on to say, "This weakness may well be the flip side of a corresponding strength."[3] In what ways could you help the church planter see his strengths as the pathway for development?

Strengths help us overcome our weaknesses, so start there. Begin by identifying and celebrating strengths so that the planter can see the potential for growth ahead. If a planter obsesses over weaknesses, a lack of self-confidence or self-awareness—or a practical misunderstanding of grace—could be the reason. Help him identify the heart issue causing the obsession.

2. Ask questions that move toward action. There is nothing worse than having a development issue revealed if a plan to grow doesn't follow. Questions like these will help the church planter think about possibilities and plans rather than seeing the issues as insurmountable obstacles:

- What could you do?
- Who is good at what you want to attempt?
- When could you talk to them?
- What resources will you need in order to be successful?
- What further actions could you take to help you develop in this area?

Practice 3: I coach the planter back to previous principles learned during training.

Church planters are not only assessed these days, but they are also trained under some of the most effective training ever. Principle after principle is passed along to them in multiple formats.

Careful thought and action items must be related to principles learned in training. If not, training is simply an informational gateway the planter must endure to get to the next stage.

The Planting Coach understands he is not a trainer. Coaching is different from training. The training phase is complete; now the planter moves to the implementation phase. Coaching leads to specific action, follow-up, and accountability. Coaching complements training by closing the learning loop through implementation.

Multiply Training is one of the training paths for the Send Network. Multiply Training is based on twelve Leadership Competencies for planters to develop. Planters face the tension of wanting to move to something new, particularly if they are frustrated with their current level of success. We remind our Multiply Coaches:

> Coaching complements training by closing the learning loop through implementation.

Your goal as a Multiply Church Planter Coach is to help the planter revisit a competency in each coaching session. During the "revisit," encourage the planter you are coaching to discuss the intended outcomes, evaluate necessary adjustments, and consider the current level of focus needed.

The repetition of revisiting a proven planter training system is more important than the next new planting idea. However planters are being trained, you can apply a similar coaching model to the principles. Below are examples of questions to help planters review and further implement Multiply Training:

1. **Calling:** How might your calling relate to your current challenges?
2. **Character:** What areas of leading yourself would you like to focus on today?
3. **Missional Engagement:** What steps could you take in the next two weeks to better understand the makeup of your community?
4. **Vision:** How have you made your vision clear? What steps could you take to make it clearer?

5. **Bold Faith:** What risks do you need to take in your leadership? Who do you know who could pray with you about that?
6. **Values:** What values do you need to focus on in the next thirty, sixty, and ninety days?
7. **Fundraising:** What is going well in your fundraising strategy? What could you do to improve your fundraising strategy?
8. **Disciple-Making:** What steps are you taking to create a disciple-making culture?
9. **Systems and Structure:** What systems are working? What systems might need more development?
10. **Team Building:** Who on your team needs your attention right now? What steps do you need to take to empower others on your team?
11. **Communication:** What in your communication is clear? What would make your communication better?
12. **Multiplication:** What would you like multiplication to look like in your church in five years? What steps will you need to take to move toward that goal?

Practice 4: I ask questions aimed toward specific church planting behaviors.

In any endeavor, your behaviors will move you away from the task at hand or move you toward the goals and vision you have set forth. Church planting and planters are no exceptions. Behaviors do not always influence outcomes, but they are part of being faithful.

Coaches come alongside a church planter and ask questions that help the planter focus on his actions as well as his heart. Proverbs speaks of the reality of our heart's determining effect on our behaviors: "Guard your heart above all else, for it determines the course of your life" (Prov. 4:23 NLT).

The task of church planting can feel overwhelming and insurmountable. If the planter does what is necessary and possible, he will find himself, through the power of God, doing what seems impossible. Coaches can be a help in this process by helping the church planter aim in the right direction with the right behaviors. The following questions are examples of coaching toward behaviors:

1. How are you cultivating relationships with people far from God?
2. What are the next steps needed in those relationships?
3. How are you encouraging disciples to cultivate these types relationships?
4. What steps can you take to communicate your vision and mission to your team?
5. What steps can you take to communicate your vision and mission to your church?

Questions like these will help you coach a church planter to do what is necessary—and move to doing what seems impossible.

Practice 5: I keep current with planting practices by reading blogs, books, etc.

Church planters have unique dreams, aspirations, and tasks. Coaches must keep learning to relate to church planters and understand their thoughts. If you are planting, don't assume you are drinking from the same information wells. If you planted years ago or if you are coming from other roles, keep learning. Here are four tips to help you keep current with church planter practices and always keep learning:

1. Ask the church planters you coach about their favorite blogs and books.
2. Ask the church planters you coach about their favorite podcasts.
3. Ask the church planters you coach about who has had the greatest impact on them as a husband, father, pastor, and planter.
4. Attend a church planting conference or seminar and learn with church planters.

Keeping current will help you serve the church planters you coach so they can fulfill their unique kingdom assignment.

The Planting Coach

Part of the framework for church planter coaching involves the church planter in pursuit of his unique kingdom assignment. Great coaches are passionate about how that assignment fits into the bigger picture of God's glory and the gospel. Thus, they care deeply about the outcome. A coach embraces his role as a helper who walks beside the planter, coaching toward church planting outcomes and behaviors.

Check the statements that best describe your coaching.

	The Practices of the Planting Coach
	I ask questions aimed toward specific church planting outcomes.
	I coach toward development issues identified during the assessment process.
	I coach the planter back to previous principles learned during training.
	I ask questions aimed toward specific church planting behaviors.
	I keep current with church planting practices by reading blogs, books, etc.

Be Coached . . .

1. What *could* you do to grow in this coaching quality?

2. What *will* you do to grow in this quality?

3. Who could help you?

My Coach Helps . . .

My coach helps me to understand some of the nuts and bolts of church planting. He was able to help me identify some pitfalls of getting a church plant off the ground and to help me in really practical, meaningful ways. It has been helpful to have someone guide me through the early stages of the church planting process and share their experiences as well.

Adam Kern
The Vine Church
Schnecksville, Pennsylvania
www.thevinechurchpa.com

CHAPTER 14

The Growing Coach

My dentist is one of my favorite people. But don't misread my enthusiasm to mean I love what he does to me. A Google search reveals how people feel about the entire dental experience. Words like *hate*, *anxiety*, and *fear* are the most common descriptions. I can relate.

A dentist from Toronto owns the web domain www.hatedentists.com. He showed great empathy through his "Top 10 Reasons People Hate Dentists" blog post. Reasons included "The Needle," "The Pain," "The Drill," and "The Lectures."[1]

Finding a new dentist is a challenge, but ours is the best. We have great conversations every time I see him. He asks questions about my recent travels and how my workouts are going. He listens to my answers and asks more questions. We always discuss our latest football opinions, and he asks about my family.

My dentist is generous. In spite of managing two local offices, he volunteers to help people in our community without insurance or adequate incomes. He is committed to his family, and all his staff respects him.

But you know why he is my dentist? My dentist has skills, and we enjoy the health benefits. My family's dental work is provided with minimal pain and discomfort. He has a great "chair-side manner," but that alone is not enough. Skills matter, right?

Skills are as important for coaches as they are for dentists. Great coaching starts with the heart of the coach—and his personal commitment to growing in Christ. Listening, asking great questions, and caring contribute to his chair-side manner. But a passion to improve his skills is essential. Great coaches possess a combination of heart and skill.

Steve Kersh directed coaching at the North American Mission Board prior to my assignment. Together we worked crafting an internal coaching definition for our mission organization. Steve helped me gain clarity while we worked. He was passionate about including two important words:

1. Intentional: Coaching relationships are unique because we are relating together for specific outcomes. Coaching is business—for God and with God. If our meetings do not end in action items for the planter, coaching didn't happen.

2. Skilled: Coaching is simple, but not easy. A great coach possesses a unique blend of heart and skill. Every coach does not have equal skills and experiences. All coaches bring certain valuable skills and experiences to a relationship, regardless of their training. Great coaches, however, are passionate about growing their coaching skills.

The following story provides a great example of an intentional, skilled relationship:

Pastor of Teaching, Vision, and Coaching

Cultivate Church was started in 2010 by Pastor Jay Francoeur and his wife, Mandy, in Voorhees, New Jersey: "All we knew was that we were being led as His family into a new future. That future included a vision of being the kind of church that was a blessing to its neighbors in the name of Jesus."[2]

Jay believes in the effectiveness of coaching both in his life and in the lives of other church planters. His title on his church website is Pastor of Teaching, Vision, and Coaching.

Jay's coaching system is working for the planters he coaches. The consistency of answering the same questions each month and forming action plans based on each coaching conversation is helping planters stay focused and healthy in the midst of the stresses of planting a church.

Coaching as an "intentional, skilled" relationship is demonstrated by how Jay coaches. He created a coaching process to coach planters effectively. His system is comprised of three parts: pre-coaching questions, the actual coaching conversations, and calendar-based action items.

Part One: Pre-coaching Questions

Questions sent in advance help planters think on their own as they process goals and obstacles. Jay can see into their situation in advance and use their time more efficiently when they meet. He uses the same questions each meeting:

- What evidences of God's grace are you celebrating right now in your group/church?
- What is a challenge you are facing that is keeping your group/church from being all that you hoped for?
- What is the mission of your group/church?
- What obstacles are you facing as a group when it comes to being effective on that mission?
- What resources might you be lacking (either human or material) that you think would help meet these challenges and enable you to better lead and serve your group?
- What would you like to spend time on in our next coaching session?
- What are one or two things, if we were able to address them, that would make you feel like the time was well spent?

Part Two: Coaching Session

Jay begins with prayer to model dependency on the Holy Spirit for insight and direction. Leaders are invited to give God thanks for the evidence of His grace since the last session.

He then leads planters through the G.O.O.D. coaching process: Goals, Obstacles, Options, and Do. Planters determine action items related to their goals and plans, along with a time line for completion.

Jay also recaps each coaching session, asking those coached to verbalize the solution(s) they believe the Spirit has led them to and the actions they will take as a result. Then they pray together to commit those plans to the Lord and ask for His help to implement them.

Part Three: Calendar-Based Action Items

Jay uses a shared document that captures action items identified during each coaching session. The document also includes completion dates attached to each item. This document helps him follow up in the next coaching conversation.

God is using Jay to coach people in his church and church planters as well. Jay models great intentional coaching skills. He remains passionate about growing as a coach. Jay said, "I don't think I have perfected this by any means, and I'd love to learn all I can!"

Jay offers planters more than a great conversation, although that is an important part of what he does. Every planter needs a coach like Jay who is highly intentional, skilled and committed to coaching excellence.

On your quest to advance as a Growing Coach, consider the following five practices:

Five Practices of the Growing Coach

Practice 1: I ask open-ended questions.

Often, the most powerful statements are questions. Jesus started a story with the question, "What do you think?" (Matt. 21:28). He asked the mother of the sons of Zebedee, "What do you want?" (Matt. 20:21). He asked a blind man, "What do you want me to do for you?" (Mark 10:51). How stunning is that? Imagine Jesus asking you these questions. How would you answer? Open-ended questions accomplish what their name suggests. The number of potential answers is unlimited.

> Often, the most powerful statements are questions.

Closed questions give you two possible answers: "yes" or "no." The negative result of closed questions in a coaching conversation is that they stop the thinking process of the planter you coach.

Martin Copenhaver describes the value of an open-ended question:

> The answer to an open-ended question is not obvious or implied. For this reason, an open-ended question can expand our thinking. The answer to an open-ended question, such as those Jesus asks, can also change over time, so it helps to keep such a question continually before you.[3]

Here are examples of open and closed questions:

Closed: Are you going to do this?
Open: What are you going to do?

Closed: Will you work on this project today?
Open: What would you like to work on today?

Closed: Will you talk to them about this problem?
Open: What is your next step to help solve this problem?

Open-ended questions help us see what God is doing and hear what God is saying by expanding our field of view, exploring His perspective, and illuminating His plans. In contrast, closed questions shut the coaching conversation down very quickly.

Consider these ways to leverage the power of open-ended questions:

- **Explore with "What."** "What would you like to work on?"
- **Expand with "W" questions.** Use "what," "who," "where," and "when" to begin your questions.
- **Plan with "How."** How *could* you move forward? How *will* you move forward?

- **Respect the power of "Why."** "Why" questions can expose opportunities concealed beneath the ordinary, beyond the ineffective, or behind the failures.

Practice 2: I know the names of the spouse and children of planters I coach.

People endure. Problems, processes, and projects are temporary. A coach values the planter he coaches by being fully present in conversations intended to work through their priorities.

How does it look to care for others? Here are three ways to care for those you coach:

1. Ask about their spouses and children by name. How are they doing? What are they celebrating? One way to learn people's names is by using them often—that takes discipline and focus. Resist the temptation to ask "How is your wife?" "How are your children?" Those names are safer and easier to remember than their real names, but are impersonal and lazy. Pronounce names correctly as well. For years the only people who pronounced my name correctly were my mother, father, and sister. That did not offend me; I mispronounce names as well. But when someone makes an effort, I notice.

2. Keep notes of family details. I learned something simple and profound after my team spent an hour with a memory expert. As much I would love a memorization trick, there is none. Focus and discipline are what make a great memory. We must decide that people are worth getting to know and be willing to do the necessary work it takes.

3. Pray for family details. Traditionally we have used the words "I remembered you in prayer" or have asked people to "Remember me when you pray." Paul describes his prayers for his spiritual family throughout his thirteen letters using similar words. "When I pray I think of you" is the essence of what he communicated. Whom do you think of when you pray? What a humbling thought—that at the most spiritually intimate part of another believer's day, I come to mind. May that be true about the planters you coach.

- Pray specifically for the planter's family.
- Pray for issues mentioned in conversation.
- Ask the planter how the Father has answered prayers.

Practice 3: I evaluate my coaching after every conversation.

God riveted a verse in my thinking, not in depths where its influence is subtle, but on the surface, commanding attention. It invokes confidence in the One who demonstrates in life: "I am at work right here, right now!"

> For it is God who works in you, both to will and work for his good pleasure. (Phil. 2:13)

A coaching relationship creates opportunities for providential moments. I remember great coaching God-moments with my coaches. I have shared many of those moments in this book. When I am coached, my self-awareness increases. I hear myself talk, I measure my words, and I see myself act.

When these components are present in our coaching conversations—a motivated planter, a skilled coach, and the Holy Spirit—the result will be God-moments. Details, goals, and plans will pass away, but God-moments will endure. Each conversation is significant, and that is why I evaluate coaching conversations with awe.

How is the planter I coach seeing the Father at work? How can I more effectively help a church planter hear God and craft powerful plans? As you evaluate your church planter coaching, here are some questions you can ask that will help you coach well:

Ask yourself:

- Did we achieve the agreed-upon outcome of the conversation?
- How closely did I follow my planter's agenda?
- What were my best questions?
- What will I do differently next time?
- What did God do today?

Check in with your planter:

- How could I be a better coach for you?
- What would make our time more valuable for you?
- How have our conversations been helpful for you?
- What is God saying?

When you see what God can do through you as a coach, your passion to evaluate will grow. You should steward your coaching moments as precious opportunities for the planter to meet with God.

Practice 4: I hold the planter I coach accountable through honest conversations.

Casper Milquetoast was a comic strip character from the 1920s. Milquetoast was famously shy, weak, and timid. His name lives on as a way to describe a person who embodies Milquetoast's character.[4]

Coaching seems like a Milquetoast approach to some. Yes, a coach is a companion, a friend, and one who lets the planter set the agenda. But the nature of a real coaching conversation involves a high level of responsibility and accountability.

When a leader is complaining too much about the people who are obstacles to progress, one question is critical. This question works for the rich, poor, young, or old:

What are you going to do?

Church planter coaches specialize in helping planters master personal responsibility. Essentially, a disciple does two things: hear God and obeys. Nothing is more encouraging and empowering for a disciple than clarifying God's will and bringing it into reality to the best of their ability.

Coaches help church planters clarify: "What do you believe God wants you to do?" Then planters pursuing God's plans craft steps to move forward.

Coaches help church planters evaluate: "How did you decide God wants you to do this?" Accountability in coaching conversations is as natural as breathing, but unlike breathing, it must be intentional.

Church planters grow stronger by holding themselves accountable to plans they have made. You will grow stronger as a church planter coach as you hold your planter accountable through honest coaching conversations.

> *Church planter coaches specialize in helping planters master personal responsibility.*

Practice 5: I have an ongoing developmental plan for my coaching skills.

Whether he is coaching one church planter or five, the Growing Coach has an ongoing developmental plan to improve his coaching skills. In Appendix B you will find a "Great Coaching Development Guide." This guide will help you create a plan based on the ten qualities of a great coach. But a plan is just a plan unless you implement it: great coaches practice effective coaching skills.

Two elements of my most recent developmental plan were:

1. Coaching to the Heart. I was in a coaching rut, always coaching through goals and action items. Even though I was aware of the danger, I had lost focus. So I made a more conscious effort to ask heart questions like: "What is really happening?" "What is God saying?" "What does God want?" I listened for key words like *concern* and *fear,* attempting to move past behaviors and tactics to the heart of the leader.

2. Using "Series" Goals in Coaching. I began to look at coaching conversations as belonging in a series, not as a string of one-off discussions. This is a concept I learned from Keith Webb (www.keithwebb.com).

For example, if I had four conversations planned with the person I was coaching, I helped the person I coached look at all four together. Then I asked questions like: "Over the next two months, what would you like to accomplish through our four conversations?"

I reviewed series goals in each conversation and asked how the person being coached felt about his progress. I would also ask how I could improve my coaching to help make their series goals. I think this was a great upgrade. One positive outcome of the series approach was that we didn't get as bogged down in small day-to-day details and were able to work on bigger things.

Your goals will be different. As you work through each of the ten qualities of a great coach, you have three "Be Coached" questions to help you design action items. But you cannot likely work on ten things at once. So reduce your list to three to five actions. Then:

- Make actions as measurable as possible.
- Talk to someone else, preferably a coach, to keep you accountable.
- Evaluate your progress in these specific areas after each coaching conversation.

Include these four elements in your plan to become a great coach:

1. **Coach.** When I started coaching, I coached everything that moved. Tell your friends you are learning to coach. Logging coaching hours is critical to your development.
2. **Be coached.** Being coached will help you grow your skill as a church planter coach. Find a peer coach and schedule four to eight regular conversations over the next two months.
3. **Ask questions.** The most natural time to ask questions is when meeting someone new. Determine to learn as much as you can about the person by asking questions. You will experience the power of authentic interest and become a better inquirer.

4. **Collaborate with coaches.** Find opportunities to talk coaching with coaches. Learn their best questions and practices. Explore ways to navigate common challenges.

Coaching is an intentional, skilled relationship. Use these practices to improve your skills and then create your own set of practices. As a result, your value to planters you coach will increase.

The Growing Coach

Great coaches are growing disciples and lifetime learners. Great coaching is a matter of the heart, but coaches want to improve their skills as well. Measuring the effectiveness of their coaching and asking for feedback from the planters they coach are routine practices.

Check the statements that best describe your coaching.

	The Practices of the Growing Coach
	I ask open-ended questions.
	I know the names of the spouse and children of the planter I coach.
	I evaluate my coaching after every conversation.
	I keep the planter accountable through honest conversations.
	I have a developmental plan for my coaching skills.

Be Coached . . .

1. What *could* you do to grow in this quality?

2. What *will* you do to grow in this quality?

3. Who could help you?

My Coach Helps . . .

My coach helps me grow in my personal life. He makes me think deeper into strategies pertaining to my current church plant. He encourages and challenges me in areas of my marriage to help us grow spiritually.

Bryce Woerner
Revive Wildwood
Wildwood, New Jersey
www.revivewildwood.com

Review the Ten Qualities of a Great Coach

Serving: *I enjoy helping others succeed in life and ministry.*

Believing: *I am confident in God's ability to transform people.*

Listening: *I give the gift of listening.*

Cheering: *I celebrate large and small wins.*

Praying: *I embrace the Holy Spirit's work in a church planter.*

Pressing: *I understand the next step is the most important one.*

Supporting: *I believe there's no one-size-fits-all formula for success.*

Relating: *I engage coaching relationships with patience and persistence.*

Growing: *My goal is to become a great coach.*

Planting: *I help church planters pursue their unique kingdom assignment.*

- What are your top three qualities?
- How can you improve your top qualities?
- What three qualities need the most work?
- How can you improve your qualities that need work?
- What actions can you take in the next thirty days to improve your coaching?

PART 3

Deliver Great Coaching

Domino's did not start as a pizza company; they started as a delivery company. Tom and James Monaghan purchased DomiNick's Pizza store, and they changed the name to Domino's. James decided to sell his share of the company back to Tom in exchange for an old Volkswagen, and the rest is history.

If you walk into Domino's headquarters in Ann Arbor, Michigan, your first discovery will be their latest innovation proudly on display: a customized delivery vehicle. Russell Weiner, president of Domino's, explained their rationale:

> At one point in America, there was no pizza delivery. We were the first. We wanted to create something that didn't exist before. We just asked ourselves, "What would the ultimate pizza delivery vehicle look like?"

Domino's answered their question by conducting an international contest to see who could design the perfect delivery vehicle. A Chevy Spark was customized with the following delivery helps:

- Oven that heats up to 140 degrees
- An external oven door tested 25,000 times
- Capacity to hold 80 pizzas
- A console designed to carry pizza, salad, and dipping sauce

Domino's describes their innovation as "a purpose-built delivery vehicle."[1]

What Really Matters

Since 2013, Domino's has inspired me. I discovered early in the process that we did not have a coach training problem. Neither did we have a lack of coaches. Our challenge was delivery.

If delivery was the target, then a mind-set shift was needed. The meaning of the word *coach* needed to move from a role we trained people to occupy. Now, *coach* means an invaluable activity that helps church planters as they pursue their unique kingdom assignment. Simply put, *coach* is a verb.

Most training and skill development programs provide better ways to approach something we already know. Upgrades are great. The desire of leaders to grow is important. Their desire is what God uses to help them lead well.

Experienced leaders often see coaching as a refreshing breakthrough. Our one-day coach orientation is learner centered and experience based. Hearing an expert lecture all day is a challenge, no matter how qualified the expert might be.

Coach orientation involves leaders talking and listening to each other. Being listened to is a rare experience for a leader. And immediately practicing the new skills they are learning is energizing.

Leaders leave coach orientation with a mind-set shift, thinking of all the new ways coaching will help them develop leaders and make disciples. Coaching is not merely a better way to approach ministry; for most of us, it has been a *new* way.

In chapter 1 we began with the kingdom as a significant part of our coaching platform. We established that every leader needs a coach, and every church planter is a leader. So the Domino's question applies (with a little contextual adaptation):

What would ~~the~~ ultimate ~~pizza~~ coaching delivery look like?

"Perfect" makes me as uncomfortable as "great" did when I first considered adding it to the word *coaching*. But remember the principle—even if the words *perfect* and *great* are challenging words, they are much better than good enough. At times, our best is as small as five loaves and two fish; but fully given to God, they can be incredibly useful.

My coaching journey included a series of "a-ha" moments and incredible discoveries. I know now that many of those came directly from the Father. At the end of a coaching call with a leader from Georgia, I experienced a breakthrough. I remember telling my wife, Yvette, "I can do this. God can use me to help people. But I can help others do this, too."

> And I am sure of this, that he who began a good work in you will bring it to completion at the day of Jesus Christ. (Phil. 1:6)

Of all my attempts to serve God, I knew I had found a new sweet spot in ministry. I remember ten years earlier hearing about something in a leader's life called "convergence." Normally this happens in a leader's fifties or sixties. Convergence is when all experiences God gives a leader converge into one. The result is a seismic discovery of "this is why I am here."[2]

I loved the convergence idea but was skeptical it would ever happen to me. But with coaching, that is what God did for me. I want the kingdom to benefit from *your* coaching discovery.

The discovery may not be as dramatic as mine, nor does it have to be. I want you to develop more coaches in your world. You cannot possibly coach everyone who needs a coach, right? Every church planter in North America needs a great coach, like the one you are becoming. His planting wife needs one as well. Let's get to work coaching and developing coaches who coach! Let's design the ultimate coaching delivery system.

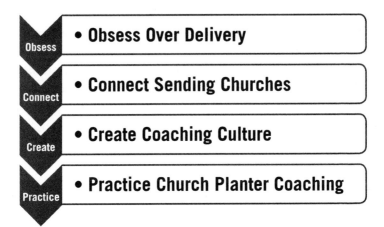

The meaning of the word *coach* must evolve from training to action. Coach is a verb, and supporting church planters is the desired outcome. Part 3 of *Sending Well* explores four vital elements of a coaching delivery system.

 **CHAPTER 15**

Obsess over Delivery

We live in a sports-crazed world. Canadians love ice hockey, Mexicans love soccer, Cubans love baseball, and the USA loves American football.[1] Although the preferred sport varies, the passion for sport is universal. The passion for sport goes far beyond wearing team colors and office debates:

> Wars have been started over it, cities set aflame because of it. Treasuries have been emptied, marriages ended, murders committed.[2]

The creation and evolution of these games over the past century are fascinating. How did they get so popular? The answer may surprise you. Marketing, brightly colored uniforms, or impressive mascots would be my thoughts. But this is not necessarily the case.

The establishment of clear written rules escalated the popularity of the sports. What are the boundaries? How do you play? How do you score and—more important—conquer your opponent?

No matter the quality of the field or equipment, a little boy with a ball made out of tape and a stick could become a baseball hero. Anyone anywhere could play and enjoy the game because the rules are simple.

Rules are not without controversy, opinions, and interpretations. In fact, how many times have you blamed the loss of your favorite team on a bad call or no call by the referee? We have mixed feelings about rules, except when they benefit our team.

Walter Camp is considered the father of American football. But ironically, he did not invent football. He took a brutal sport and systematized the rules. As hazardous as American football is now, when soccer and rugby combined in the 1860s, it was worse. Nineteen college students were killed playing college football in 1905.[3]

Gary Belsky and Neil Fine described Walter Camp's influence on the sport:

> American football, like other emerging sports of the time, wasn't played the same way everywhere and would likely have faded into history without a set of mutually agreed rules.[4]

Creating Coaching Rules Is the First Step

Leaders like to make their rules when it comes to coaching church planters. But those in a healthy church planter coaching system see the bigger picture of delivering great coaching to every church planter. To measure quality and make coaching great, a mutually agreed-upon set of rules is vital.

Coaching must happen the same way everywhere—but don't let that scare you. Rules are boundaries that coaches appreciate. How to score and how to win at church planter coaching are important. Similar to you watching football on Saturday or Sunday, boundaries clear the path to use your skills. Rules or boundaries make the coaching relationships better; they don't create robots.

A customized coaching relationship would have advantages for certain planters but not all. But there would be limitations to this approach to church planter coaching. Most planters are resourceful. They are good at finding the help they want but not always the help they need. A consistent coaching presence in every planter's life that addresses both felt needs and actual needs is important. Here is why:

1. A church planter's understanding of his needs is limited.

The statement "People don't know what they don't know" is true. A coach could meet the felt needs of a church planter but possibly miss his actual needs. Self-awareness is a challenge to any leader—church planters and coaches included. Paul Tripp describes our condition: "There is no one we swindle more than we swindle ourselves. There is no one we run to defend more than we do ourselves."[5] We all discover our weaknesses over time, but a blind spot is called a blind spot because we don't know it is there.

2. The number of qualified coaches is limited.

We idealize the most helpful coach as one who has been there, done that, and is uniquely qualified to help anyone do the same thing. In most areas, that coaching profile is difficult to find, particularly if we are attempting to give each planter his own coach.

Successful, respected practitioners working with groups of planters are invaluable. Since their number is limited, we can better steward their influence as strategic coaches with groups of planters. A shepherding coach is different than a strategic coach. His skills bring value to church planters as well. The platform is a one-on-one, abiding relationship.

> How can we create meetings that produce a high return on investment for every planter and his family?

The church planter process will not fit into neat columns like the one below. Group coaches can address personal and family issues. One-on-one coaches can address church issues. But the environments can be complementary, and both are necessary for a healthy approach to sending well.

The danger of overwhelming planters with meetings is real. But the solution is not simply eliminating meetings. Great meetings that help planters move faster and further are worth every minute invested. In sales terms, the value of the meetings must outweigh the cost of attending. So the question for those who facilitate meetings in both columns is: *How can we create meetings that produce a high return on investment for every planter and his family?*

	Strategic Coach	**Shepherd Coach**
Meetings	Networks/Groups	One-on-One
Frequency	6–8 times yearly	12–16 times yearly
Advantages	Best practices; strategic next steps; skill development; group support	Personal and customized; safer environment for self-disclosure
Outcomes	Skills and strategy development	Personal and spiritual formation
Qualifications	Track record of planting success; lifetime learner	Fully engaged in God's mission; trained; committed to abide
Delivery	More helped in less time; fewer coaches needed; meetings are already happening in many areas; smaller pool of qualified coaches	More credible coaches needed; length of commitment is greater; skills more easily reproducible; larger pool of qualified coaches
Focus	Plant, Planter, Family	Planter, Family, Plant

3. The most qualified coaches want to do things their way.

We want to set coaches up for success. Also, we want to give them a fair estimate of the time needed to invest in a planter through coaching. If each coach does everything according to his personal preference, you will never have a healthy system for all coaches and planters.

Coaches need to be multiplied. Customized approaches to coaching are impossible to scale (grow) or sustain (endure). Also, coaches help coaches grow. A brotherhood among coaches builds trust among planters that coaches have their best interest at heart.

4. Great coaching is always customized.

Does that feel like a contradiction? As coaches, we can be guilty of attempting to shape a leader into what we think he should be. Normally, we impose our ministry experience and successes on the planter, regardless of our differences.

Great coaches surrender their agendas to God. The coaching relationship is about the planter's gifts, strengths, vision, and context. A coach can coach any church model or context beyond his own because coaching is not about him, but about what God wants.

"We Deliver" Is the Next Step

Fred Smith's story and the creation of FedEx are famous in business folklore. Everyone who hears the story is filled with hope that one day their crazy idea might become something big.

One of FedEx's most famous marketing campaigns included a jingle with a huge promise: "We deliver. We deliver. We deliver for you." When you look closely at what Fred Smith proposed to do, you can appreciate what a crazy promise "We deliver for you" was in the beginning.

You can walk into a FedEx office in Miami, Florida, today with a package for Seattle, Washington. It will land in someone's hands in Seattle tomorrow morning. Crazy!

Every church planter deserves a crazy coaching delivery promise. If you are like me, you have overpromise phobia—get over it! Everything we do is built on the belief that no planter should plant alone. We are bound by a biblical ethic to love, support, and equip those families God sends. Together, as partners in the gospel, we say to church planters: *We want you to succeed at what the King has assigned you to do.*

If that is what you believe, then the next church planter in your city should be met with a promise: *We will deliver great coaching to you.*

Hearing yourself make this promise is as important as the planter's reassurance. Say those words with fear and trembling. And may your words be used by God to inspire you to courageously recruit, develop, and train church planter coaches to help coach.

> We want you to succeed at what the King has assigned you to do.

The promise is significant, and the complexities are great. Without strong resolve and determination, you will never deliver. Your greatest challenge will be staying committed to a system with coaches who play by the rules. Utilizing a system that involves simple processes requires focus from a community of leaders.

My friend, Glenn Smith, is a business coach (www. glennsmithcoaching.com) with a strong history of helping church planters. Glenn has influenced, trained, and coached church planters for years. He knows the tension leaders feel when asked to work within a system. Leaders make their systems—and are lukewarm to following someone else's process. Glenn made a business connection:

> Leaders always want to recreate the wheel. Following a system is a mind-set they have to adopt. But you don't buy a million dollar McDonald's franchise to do it the Burger King way, or worse yet, to make up your way. McDonald's is worth one million dollars because the system works! Coaching is usually delivered poorly by coaches because they don't have a system or they don't follow their system.

Local ownership of church planter coaching is critical for a delivery system to work. Coaching delivery requires a lot of moving parts. Those parts can break at a moment's notice. If you ignore the broken parts, you will kill your coaching culture with frustrated coaches or disappointed planters. Create a team, no matter how small, to oversee and maintain the system. And create a team that will obsess over delivery.

Delivery Systems 101

Coach training is most commonly confused with coaching delivery. The false assumption is that "If we train coaches, they will coach church planters." Our one-day coach orientation is a step in the coaching process for people who have already committed to coach.

An invitation to "check out the training and then decide if you want to coach a planter" changes the tone of orientation. Prospective coaches tend to enter the room as customers instead of owners. Communicate the big picture and ask for a commitment. More work will be required upfront, but the long-term value will be greater.

Sometimes making a coaching assignment is confused with coaching delivery. For years I have seen assignments made to well-intentioned coaches, and yet the relationships never happened. For the coaching relationship to get off the ground, usually coaching leaders must make the introduction, explain the agreement, and have the coach and planter schedule at least four meetings in advance. Scheduling meetings one at a time is virtually impossible for busy leaders.

Remember, your system is not designed to deliver a coach; it is designed to deliver *coaching*. Making an assignment is a great step in the process, but coaching has not happened until the first meeting occurs. We remind our coaches: *coach* is a verb.

Systems

A *system* is a set of connected parts that work together for one outcome. My car consists of tires, brakes, horn, and an engine for one outcome: transportation. My house is made up of beds, sinks, showers, a refrigerator, stove, toilets, heating, and air conditioning for one outcome: shelter.

For a coaching delivery system to work, leaders have to keep their eye on the target. The moving parts of the system include:

Planters	Assigning coaches
Coaches	Coach development
Coaching Champion (local leader)	Resourcing coaches
Coaching conversations	Discovering coaching candidates
Coaching guides	Communicating coaching stories
Coaching reports	Sending churches
Coaching feedback from planters	Denominational missionaries
New coach orientation (training)	And more . . .

Processes

A *process* is a series of repeatable steps or actions within a system. Examples: Lather, Rinse, Repeat; Stop, Drop, Roll; Preheat, Stir, Bake.

Below are simple steps in a delivery process. Yours does not have to be identical, but they should be clear and reviewed often. You can see an illustrated version of this process in Appendix C.

Step One: Invite qualified coaches to orientation.

Step Two: One-Day Coach Orientation—coaches review principles and practices.

Step Three: Peer Coaching—coaches prepare through practice with a peer.

Step Four: Church Planter Coaching—coaches assigned and coaching planters.

Step Five: Coaching Pod—ongoing coaches' support and development.

Evaluate Your System

Utilizing the following tool helps coaching leaders keep an eye on the target: *Deliver great coaching to every church planter.* We call it a "Coaching 360" because it gives three distinct views of planter coaching in your area:

1. Assess the *Need*: How many coaches are needed?
2. Measure the *Capacity*: How many new coaches do you need?
3. Examine the *Quality*: How great is the coaching?

As you read the following section, you can do a "Coaching 360" for your area. A blank "360" form is in Appendix D.

1. Assess the Need

A1. *How many planters under two years' post-launch need coaches?*
Questions A1 and A2 create a coaching baseline. Establishing a starting point is crucial for creating your coaching system. Reduce the list based on the number of credible coaches with the capacity to coach. If you have three coaches, reduce the list to the top three planters. In this simple delivery system, coaches can be prepared to coach quickly.

A2. *How many planter deployments do you anticipate in the next twelve months?*
The newest planters go to the top of any coaching list. A year-two planter can become a year-one coach in this system. But remember, rules for coaching are critical. Coaching is a supportive relationship, not a directive one.

A3. *Total coaching relationships needed over the next twelve months:*
In a volunteer coaching system, coaches can normally only manage one coaching relationship at a time. Estimate the amount of time needed to invest in a healthy coaching relationship. Our formula is twice a month for eight months a year, or sixteen conversations.

What are the steps to help this part of your system operate efficiently?

Example: Connect with each church planter in your pipeline to get an update on their plans, including an estimated start date.

2. Measure the Capacity

M1. *How many competent coaches do you have with the capacity to coach a planter?*
Managing an active roster of coaches is crucial to the health of your system. Keeping them engaged in coaching is another health indicator. Chapter 2 provides more information on the characteristics of strong coaching candidates.

M2. *How many church planter coaches are actively coaching church planters?*
No matter their skills and experience, inactive coaches are an energy drain to your system. Inactive coaches are not improving their coaching skills and are missing the encouragement that comes from helping a church planter. Under no circumstances should a church planter coach be inactive. Assign them to a team member, apprentice, or intern if needed, but keep coaches coaching.

> No matter their skills and experience, inactive coaches are an energy drain to your system.

M3. *Total number of new coaches needed to meet demand:*
Having a truly scalable system will support the coaching demand, whether

it is large or small. If you have two new planters coming to your city, and all your current coaches are active, train two new coaches. Orient them informally over two extended lunch meetings. And let these new coaches know of their importance to God and His kingdom.

M4. *We have a delivery process for the orientation of new coaches. Yes/No*

Think about the basics of coaching and resist the temptation to answer questions coaches are yet to ask. Outline your orientation meeting in steps that best describe your coaching process. What are the basics of coaching a church planter? Steve Addison created the best simple orientation guide to coaching via his *Startup Guide to Coaching Leaders.*[6]

What are the steps to help this part of your system operate efficiently?

Example: Create a database with the name of each competent coach in my area and connect with them to see if they are coaching.

3. Examine the Quality

E1. *Coaching conversations have predetermined agendas.*

Predetermined agendas are an asset to great coaching. A series of questions give both the coach and the planter coached an easy way to prepare for the conversation beforehand. The coaching conversation begins with an email prompt to answer five to ten simple questions. When the person coached returns their answers, the conversation continues. Coaches can pray, take notes, and prepare second-level questions. On meeting day, the conversation is already well underway.

E2. *The number of coaching meetings is prescribed.*

The coaches are vetted and assigned; the planters are ready to be coached, so all the work is done, right? Wrong—the real work begins after the assignments are made. The biggest challenge in coaching is to meet consistently. Research has proven that the number of times a coach meets with the person they coach and how often they meet are the keys to successful coaching.

E3. *The number of coaching meetings is reported.*
I love the coaching reports of the Baptist Convention of Maryland-Delaware. Coaches are asked to report the "pulse" of the planter as well as the number of meetings. Church Planter Catalyst Marcus Redding oversees coaching for the region. Reports can be as simple as "we met twice this month." Reports can be included in a standard church planter report by adding three simple questions:

1. How many times did you meet with your coach this month?
2. How did your coach help you?
3. What could make your coaching more fruitful?

E4. *Our current coaches have developmental plans.*
Part of building a positive coaching culture is promoting your assignable coaches' commitment to personal growth. The first step in promoting their commitment to growth is keeping them accountable to have a growth plan. Appendix B has a survey for a coach to self-assess based on the "Ten Qualities of a Great Coach." A Great Coaching Development worksheet helps coaches create a short-term plan to improve.

> *Part of building a positive coaching culture is promoting your assignable coaches' commitment to personal growth.*

E5. *We survey our coached planters twice a year for coaching quality feedback.*
Building trust in a church planter coaching system is critical. The planters will initially wonder what the real motivation is for being assigned a coach.

Is the network or denomination trying to protect their investment and reputation? Is the coach there to help or to manage a planter?

One way to build trust is to request feedback from the planters consistently. A simple survey tool is not only an easy way to gain feedback, but it also provides safe storage and easy retrieval for coaching leaders.

Consistent reporting from the planters and coaches helps you evaluate the effectiveness of your system. Ask three to five simple, open-ended questions. Keep questions as positive as possible to get more valuable responses. Here are a few examples:

- What specific ways did your coach help you over the past six months?
- What goals did you accomplish through coaching?
- What is one thing that would make coaching more valuable to you?
- How could we help our coaches improve?

Warning: Review feedback and make appropriate adjustments to your system. If you are not ready or able to do so, don't ask. Ignoring feedback erodes confidence in your system.

What are next steps to help this part of your system operate efficiently?

Example: Design a simple online survey to send to each planter at the end of this semester.

Next Steps to Upgrade the Quality of Your Church Planter Coaching System:

Goal:	Time Line:
Goal:	Time Line:
Goal:	Time Line:
Goal:	Time Line:
Goal:	Time Line:

Be Coached . . .

1. What were your highlights from this chapter?

2. What one step do you need to take immediately?

3. What are your current rules for coaching?

4. How can you add more structure to your coaching?

My Coach Helps . . .

For the past year I have met with my coach via FaceTime, and he has helped me see how to employ missional communities in the life of our church. He has encouraged me when mission seems to be in a slow season, helping me to see how I can better use that season to equip my people. Additionally, it's been great to simply have someone to bounce ideas off of and ask what I could be doing better as I try to reach people with the gospel.

Derek Van Ruler
Sunbury City Church
Sunbury, Pennsylvania
www.sunburychurch.com

 **CHAPTER 16**

Value Sending Churches

Sending a man into space was relatively new in 1962. The Soviet Union sent the first man into space in 1961 at a time when the U.S. had only sent unmanned satellites and chimpanzees. The following month, a *Mercury 7* astronaut, Alan Shepard, became the first American sent into space.

The Sending Investment

Between 1961 and 1964, the budget of the National Aeronautics and Space Administration (NASA) increased 500 percent. The NASA workforce included 34,000 full-time employees and 375,000 contractors.[1] Astronauts were icons in American culture. But without the enormous budget and workforce committed to sending man into space, none of this would have happened.

In 1962 John Glenn was the first American to orbit the earth. Glenn's last trip into space was at the age of seventy-seven as part of the space shuttle *Discovery* in 1998.

National Public Radio provided their perspective on Glenn after his death:

> Astronaut, Senator, national hero—that's how we're remembering John Glenn. He died yesterday at the age of 95. If John Glenn had never left his hometown of New Concord, Ohio, he'd likely still be extraordinary, just on a smaller stage. But because he left, we all got to soar a little higher.[2]

John Glenn and the Apostle Paul

As you think about the vastness of NASA and its mission, you can connect something even greater. Astronauts like John Glenn and others were the heroes and celebrities of NASA. But without the talents, gifts, and resources of thousands, if not millions, more, John Glenn would have never left the ground.

> God's mission is the greatest sending operation in history.

God's mission is the greatest sending operation in history. Sending well is a hands-on endeavor of many. Sent ones, like Paul and Barnabas, are famous. But they are only one part of the equation—if sending well is the target. For Paul and Barnabas to leave the smaller stage, a high level of investment by the Antioch Church was crucial.

Local Churches Should Surrender Their Best Leaders

Picture a true apostle-entrepreneur on your church staff or as a disciple in your church. He is always pressing, always a contrarian, with a new and better way to push into the blue ocean of lostness. "We're just not doing this right" is his mantra.

This apostle is an independent thinker shackled by the localization of his ministry and church. Wrapping his brain or heart around your legitimate sending concerns is impossible. They are trivial to him, but not to you.

Imagine Paul as your associate pastor, chairman of deacons, elder, or small group leader. Called by some the "greatest Christian who ever lived," he has endeared himself to billions of Christ-followers throughout the centuries.

Here is the Antioch solution: Send your best Barnabas (son of encouragement) with your best Paul to keep him encouraged. And trust God to use sending to glorify Himself and extend the gospel's influence outside your local pond.

The diverse leadership team of Antioch—Paul and Barnabas included—was praying, fasting, and worshiping God when they decided to send. We see the Holy Spirit in the middle of the local situation saying, "I know what you should do. Send them!"

The highlights:

> Then after fasting and praying they laid their hands on them and sent them off. So, being sent out by the Holy Spirit, they went down to Seleucia, and from there they sailed to Cyprus. (Acts 13:3–4)

> And from there they sailed to Antioch, where they had been commended to the grace of God for the work that they had fulfilled. And when they arrived and gathered the church together, they declared all that God had done with them, and how he had opened a door of faith to the Gentiles. And they remained no little time with the disciples. (Acts 14:26–28)

The Summary

1. God had a unique kingdom assignment for Paul and Barnabas.
2. Barnabas was as important a part of the sending mission as Paul.
3. The Holy Spirit and the Antioch Church were fully engaged co-senders.
4. Antioch's loss was the kingdom's gain.
5. The assignment bore spiritual fruit: "a great number of both Jews and Greeks believed" (Acts 14:1).
6. Paul and Barnabas returned to Antioch for a report and celebration time.

The local church has a difficult choice. Do we imprison all our best leaders, resisting the divine impulse to release them? Do we hold on to them to make one locality the center of the universe? Or will we have an equal passion for sending and keeping?

The Antioch Church released two of their best leaders, obeying the outward, multidirectional push of the Holy Spirit. In Acts 1:8, Jesus predicted things like this would happen. Our natural inclination may be to hold on to every asset to make a local church great, but the gospel was never intended to stay in one place.

Co-senders: The Local Church and the Holy Spirit

The Antioch story highlights the unique roles of co-senders. The leaders of the Antioch Church "laid their hands on them and *sent* them" (Acts 13:3, emphasis mine). No matter how large and effective our denominational missions and parachurch organizations become, the local church is more important.

Delivering God's mission without the local church as the central sender is inadequate and mutated. Pat Hood said, "Churches have a responsibility to be part of sending people and staying involved in their lives. . . . The health of God's mission depends on it."[3]

Our resources and power to influence the nations have limits, no matter how many churches are involved. The natural supply of leaders, money, and strategy will one day disappear. The church can release all their people and financial assets to the kingdom, but they cannot empower. Church planting is more than personnel and funds.

Paul and Barnabas were released by the local church but were "sent out by the Holy Spirit" (Acts 13:4). The word and image are different for "sent" when the Holy Spirit does the sending.

- The Holy Spirit sends out—with the force of a strong, inexplicable wind.
- The local church sets free—they pray, release, and support.

Both senders are vital to God's mission; but both have unique roles. Agencies don't send. Denominations don't send. They support and assist those who do send—beginning with the local church.

The Search for Movement Leaders

I am indebted to local churches like the Grace Baptist Church in Elizabethton, Tennessee. I came to Christ there as a boy. Missionaries from Moody Aviation who were being trained to take the gospel to the nations were my teachers. Numerous lay leaders were part of my journey, and some remain in my life more than fifty years later. Pastors poured into me and loved me enough to give me an occasional rebuke.

I served in every way imaginable, from knocking on doors to singing in the choir, as God clarified His call in my life. My peers at Grace Baptist went on to be pastors, church planters, and strong leaders in local churches.

At the ripe age of fifteen years old, I preached my first sermon at Grace. My spiritual family at Grace Baptist took care of everything. I did not disciple, teach, train, or rebuke myself; they covered all the bases. God planned to have me there.

Connecting the Dots

I struggled to connect the dots from my past to my effort to find leaders in the future. Maybe I hoped church planters would mysteriously appear in my office through a *Star Trek* transporter.

Local churches arrived on the scene almost two thousand years before my denomination. Southern Baptists were latecomers to God's party. Another realization was that leaders were drawn to life-giving churches much more than denominational entities, no matter how "cool" we thought we were. My focus shifted back to local churches, a focus that was not only biblical, but also practical.

Helping local churches become co-senders was an apostolic responsibility as denominational leaders. In fact, I struggled to justify my existence apart from an apostolic role. His glory and the gospel were at stake.

Because our denomination had grown large, we had inadvertently caused a reverse thrust that killed local church ownership of church planting. Churches gladly passed the mantle of church planting back to us.

South Carolina Baptists were generous people. Now we stood resource rich and leader poor. Another by-product of this centralized denominational approach was that most of our churches had disowned church planting. Southern Baptist statistics revealed that less than 5 percent of our churches were directly involved in church planting.

Ed Stetzer's most recent research uses a more narrow definition of direct involvement. His research revealed that 3 percent of all Protestant churches acted as the primary source of support for a new church over the previous twelve months.[4]

Since church planting was our job as a denomination, we were now responsible for any perceived negative outcomes. Church planting became highly politicized as a result. Unsuccessful new churches were our failures. New churches planted in the wrong places or that practiced the "wrong" methods were all the denomination's responsibility.

We were living in the middle of a dilemma:

- We had what we wanted (resources, empowerment).
- But we no longer wanted what we had (no leaders, no local church ownership).

Our church planting system was dysfunctional, and we were responsible. Because of an unbiblical approach to planting, our efforts were not fruitless, but they were mutated.

Our strategic shift was to church planting centers based in local churches and strong sending churches. The Cypress Project (www.cypressproject.org) was launched through North Rock Hill Church under the leadership of Pastor Chris Ruppe and Neal McGlohon. Other planting center churches soon emerged in Bluffton and Charleston.

Our new churches were required to find a sending church, and we were willing to help. My close friend, Dr. Rob White, was one of our planting strategists. His main responsibility was to discover, develop, and equip sending churches. And he was great at it.

Much to our surprise, there was a greater willingness to own church planting than we thought, and there was more ownership than we knew. God had already put sending in the hearts of church leaders.

From Mirrors to Windows

In the late eighties and nineties, I was pastor of the First Baptist Church in Marrero, Louisiana. Marrero was located on the west bank of the Mississippi River in New Orleans. Although technically considered suburban New Orleans, Marrero seemed far from the suburban life I had seen elsewhere.

Racial and economic diversity plus population density made Marrero urban. Ten miles and the Mississippi River were all that separated us from the urban core of New Orleans.

By no means did we have the intentionality, intelligence, or financial resources of NASA, but we decided to engage The Westbank as a launching pad for ministries and new churches.

Evolving from a smaller, traditional church to a "Key Church" was a journey. We already had one Vietnamese mission church when I became the pastor in 1986. Everybody wanted them to leave. I was indifferent at the time.

We were ill equipped and too spiritually immature to address the diverse and dense population of Westbank. Neither was the word *sending* part of the language we used to describe what God wanted us to do.

What we knew, however, was that God wanted us to stop looking in the mirror and start looking out the window. This may sound like a baby step to you, but for us it was epic. What we loved most at the time was meeting and eating. Painting and protecting our facilities were also high on the priority list. But God wanted us to see people differently and do what we could do to reach them with the gospel. Eventually, we began to own our responsibility for the people around us.

Key Church Strategy

I was an "in the moment" leader, but my discovery of the "Key Church" mission strategy gave us a course to follow. A Texas Baptist Convention leader, J. V. Thomas, provided a simple path to add a level of intentionality to the direction we were heading. And the strategy gave us a way to involve more people in helping new churches.

Our new identity as a Key Church was invaluable. The approach provided metrics for us to consider. We approached our goals with a startup golfer's mentality—we used our previous score as the score to beat. One thing I was intuitively good at doing was celebrating small wins, and because our baseline in missional engagement was so low, early wins were easy.

The Key Church Strategy presented three pathways. The bronze level meant we would have a volunteer Minister of Missions and a Missions Development Council to plan our new initiatives. Our goals were to initiate one new church and one new ministry each year. The strategy put missional engagement on a shelf we could reach.

The silver level challenged us to have a part-time Minister of Missions and begin two new churches and two new ministries each year. We learned and grew under the leadership of Dr. Alton James, from New Orleans Baptist Theological Seminary, as our Minister of Missions. We never made it to the gold level: three missions and ministries, along with a full-time Minister of Missions.

Ownership was slow, but it happened. We connected to as many as five new local congregations at a time. Our outreach efforts included apartment ministries, work with addicts, block parties, and food ministries to the poor.

God moved us to a launching pad to send others as well as ourselves. We matured from looking in the mirror at ourselves to looking out the window at our community. We then moved outside and engaged our community with the gospel on a new level.

Sending Church Support

The sending church idea has become much more intentional and intelligent compared to our efforts in the eighties and nineties. The North American Mission Board (SBC) provides multiple entry points for churches to send. These ideas (as with Key Church) provide templates you can follow to create your version of these strategies.

Local churches are challenged to engage new churches through these steps:

1. **Pray.** Choose a city, state, or college campus. Pray for the planters in that area. Connect through newsletters and other social media outlets to pray with greater insight.
2. **Participate.** Choose a specific planter and new plant to begin a partnership. In addition to prayer, begin conversations about how a long-term supportive partnership might look. Bless the planter and his family by remembering birthdays and special occasions with gift cards.
3. **Provide resources.** Provide short-term and long-term volunteers. Take special offerings or provide monthly based on the planter's strategy and needs.
4. **Send.** Follow the Antioch church model with a high level of hands-on involvement. Take responsibility for a church plant from birth through growth, maturity, and multiplication.

Sending Churches and Coaching

Local churches are incubators for leaders, planters, and coaches. The point of this chapter is to highlight the significance of the local church as the biblical resource for all mission endeavors. Anyone can send themselves, but no one can send themselves well without the support of a sending church.

Our focus must move beyond saying "thank you" to your donor base, whether that is a few churches or a few thousand. Churches are not donors; they are owners of biblical missions. We must help deploy them.

Your best church planter coaches will come from local churches. Sorry for giving you a blazing flash of the obvious, but don't let your frustration with local churches make you miss their unique potential. Many churches that seem apathetic, uninterested, and self-centered may have never been invited to the sending party.

> Your best church planter coaches will come from local churches.

Your best church planters and church planting leaders will come from local churches. Don't wait for them to show up on your doorstep or rely on seminaries and Bible colleges as sending agencies. Keep the dots connected to the place God intended: the local church.

Your Coaching Pipeline

The pipeline for church planter coaches begins in the local church. In my early days of coaching, I was thrilled with the results I saw in the lives of leaders. But I soon discovered that I couldn't coach everybody.

Don't leave great church planter coaches unutilized while you're out enjoying your coaching relationships. Go to local churches to look for more. Keep looking for the next group of church planter coaches—and love coaches more than coaching.

Who are your next church planter coaches from local churches?

- *Church planters:* The first place everyone should look is to church planters. But don't assume that is their best place on the sending team. Planters can make great coaches. Training, assessing, and mentoring are also great roles in addition to coaching.

- *Church planters' wives for coaching planting wives:* Church planting wives are making constant adjustments. And they are often in less control of their worlds than their husbands. A strong coach can help them hear God and stay focused.

- *Church planting team members:* Team members can be better suited to coach than their pastors. They understand church planting and are often more implementers than visionaries.

- *Sending church coaches:* If the sending church invests in planting, the sending church pastor can make a great coach. But the need to wear more hats than the coaching hat will challenge his coaching effectiveness. Delegating coaching to someone else, even to a sending pastor from another church, is a great alternative. Sending church staff members and mission pastors can make great coaches. The sending church also is a great resource for coaching planting and team member wives.

- *Business professionals:* Business professionals coach planters in our system. We hope their number increases in the future. Although a coach is not an advisor, professionals' business experience gives them credibility with planters and helps them understand the challenges of leadership.

> *Train coaches in local churches, cast vision in local churches, and move them up the sending pipeline.*

- *Professional coaches in newer churches:* Strong professional coaches can coach well from any context. Professional coaches volunteer their services in our system. When they come from new churches, there is less of a learning curve. The planter may trust them more as well.

- *Pastors/staff members who have planted:* Experience in church planting adds credibility to the coach. As they understand their role, deferring to trainers and mentors as advisors, they can make great coaches.

You will never create an effective coaching delivery system without drawing coaches from local churches. Ministry ideas and initiatives always change. Without the platform of local churches, local leaders will move on to something else quickly. Train coaches in local churches, cast vision in local churches, and move them up the sending pipeline.

Be Coached . . .

1. What churches in your area are reproducing leaders?

2. What churches are reproducing churches?

3. How can you involve these churches in coaching?

4. What steps can you take to move coaching closer to local churches?

My Coach Helps . . .

My experience of being coached has revolutionized how I make decisions as a church planter. Coaching produces a multidimensional view of the tasks at hand, which results in greater productivity and a greater sense of personal fulfillment. Iron sharpens iron: coaching has sharpened my focus on fulfilling the vision God has given me as a church planter on Vancouver Island. Whether being coached or self-coaching, I can focus on what is truly important when there are so many demands on my time.

Matthew Bond
Ekklesia Baptist Church
Sidney, British Columbia Canada
www.ekklesiabc.ca

CHAPTER 17

Create a Coaching Culture

I was in a place I had never been before: unemployed. Being stuck between my secure church planting role with the South Carolina Baptist Convention and nothing was a tough place. Marshall was my supervisor and friend whom I deeply loved. He made a statement to me, with his unmistakably strong Southern drawl, that God etched in my heart:

God's got your back.

I am not implying God has a strong Southern drawl—at least I don't think He does. I have close friends in Northern America that would be deeply disappointed if they discovered He did. But I can still hear Marshall's voice when he declared, "God's got your back!"

Hard lessons are the only ones I remember. At my phase in life, I don't expect that to change. In the middle of my pain, fear, and identity crisis, God put a book in front of me called *Notes from the Coach* by my friend Ed Cerny. The book was simple but powerful.

Most of the next steps in my journey were undecided at that point. But one thing I knew: coaching was going to be a big part of the equation. Ed's book led me through his Pro-Vision process that included a simple way to create my Pro-Values.[1] Recently, I found my values handwritten in the book as per Ed's instructions and had a God-moment. Those values were my heart for coaching from before I wrote them and are what drives me today. But the God-moment for me was bigger than words scribbled on a page.

The God-moment reminded me of Marshall's words: "God's got your back!"

God's Got Your Back

What a relevant message to deliver to church planting families! Coaching must be more than a "hoop" we ask planters to jump through or a season of their journey. If church planter coaching is surrounded by all kinds of hype for a few months and then moves totally off the grid, we communicate bad values.

> **S** = See God's potential in people.
> **E** = Esteem others over yourself.
> **R** = Remember details.
> **V** = Value the ideas of people.
> **E** = Encourage people forward.

When God embeds something into people's souls, it does not go away. Coaching is about serving leaders. I don't own a T-shirt that says "Coaching Is the Way, Truth, and Life." But we all have a T-shirt that says something. I prefer "God's Got Your Back!" on mine. What an encouraging message for church planting families. Coaching is one way to communicate this message. Coaches are here to serve.

Your Coaching Culture Is Your Coaching Future

The history, behavior, and attitudes of the people in your church planting system create an undertow, and that undertow is your organizational culture. Your planting system is made up of churches in your network or in some instances one church that drives the activity. An undertow, although seldom visible to the naked eye, moves everyone in one direction or the other.

An undertow is only bad if it is taking you someplace you don't want to go. The same can be said about your organizational culture, whether it is in your church, your network of churches, or your business. Culture is the invisible environment that influences the direction of the whole. You already have a culture that is working either for or against church planter coaching.

Your coaching culture may be somewhere on the spectrum from "Coaches are not important" to "Every planter has a great coach." For coaching to become scalable (growing to meet the demand) and sustainable (permanent), your current coaching culture must be identified and influenced.

> You already have a culture that is working either for or against church planter coaching.

This chapter will provide three ideas to help create a stronger coaching culture in your city:

1. Change the Conversation
2. Create a "We" Culture
3. Be Tenacious about Great Coaching

If you are working solo, I hope you won't be for long. But these three ideas are relevant for you as well.

Change the Conversation

Dr. Carlisle Driggers was one of my former bosses in South Carolina. His influential fifteen-year tenure was marked by strong support for local churches around the vision of "Empowering Kingdom Growth." Dr. Driggers often said, "To change the culture you have to change the conversation." And that is what he did.

Create ways to change the coaching conversation in your area. Before long, the undertow will pull stronger in the right direction. The following examples will help you change the conversation.

Talk to Coaching Leaders

Your current coaching realities can be identified by conversations with key church planting leaders in your city. So the first step is to have conversations—lots of them. Ask the same questions to everybody and compare the answers. Identify the obstacles and opportunities for improving your coaching culture. The following table helps you process answers you might hear.

Identify the Coaching Culture in Your City
"We don't have any coaches; help us develop some."
"Our coaches hurt planters more than they helped."
"Every planter has a great coach."
"Only our Anglo contemporary planters have coaches."
"We are in constant communication with our coaches."
"Coaches are not important."
"Our coaches work together to provide great coaching."
"We have coaches but have no idea what they do."
"Our coaches collaborate with our trainers and assessors."
"Our coaches are expert directors."

When reading these comments, the current coaching undertow becomes clearer. Process your next steps through a series of questions like these:

- What are the positives that will make a coaching culture easy to strengthen?
- What are the challenges that will push against your efforts?
- What needs to be learned?
- What needs to be unlearned?
- What are your next steps to improving your coaching culture?

Ghosts from the past can haunt your efforts—but wins from your past can pull coaching forward. Identifying both is critical.

Define "Every" Planter

If your vision is similar to ours—deliver great coaching to every church planter—then defining "every planter" is crucial.

Local leaders must determine how long new planters need "assigned" coaches. They will always need coaching; that is not the question. The questions are:

- What is the critical season when every new planter *must* have a coach?
- What is your capacity to *provide* this coach?

We define the critical season for coaching new planters as the first two years. Admittedly, the second question is the most challenging. Providing a two-year coach taxes our coaching capacity in every city. We would love to provide a coach longer, but the first step is to hit the two-year target consistently.

Every planter also includes all ethnicities. Confession: *The picture of "church planter" in most of our minds is not consistent with realities of reaching all peoples in North America with the gospel.* Half of the churches planted by our denomination alone in the thirty-two Send Cities are non-anglo. Providing great coaching to every Anglo planter is an overwhelming challenge. But the option to master one ethnicity first and then move to another is neither viable nor biblical.

We have made progress with Hispanics and French-speaking Canadians. By God's grace we are better than we were, but not where we want to be.

Veteran missionary Brian Harper develops coaches among Hispanics. Bringing a new ministry tool like coaching into a different culture creates unique challenges. Here are Brian's challenges with Hispanic coaching:

1. An existing authority structure that operates from the top down. Hispanic culture is more conducive to mentoring. Training new coaches and helping them to see the value of a good coach that moves you to awareness and action are vital.

2. A culture that values relationships and friendships. Coaching for Hispanics works best through established relationships. But it cannot be reduced to a time merely to "hang out" or listen to a friend in the journey. Intentionality must integrate into the power of relational living and connectivity to bring about results. Clarifying the meaning of coaching is critical.

Woody Wilson is the Coaching Champion and a partner-supported missionary in Quebec. Woody applauds the coachable spirit he has discovered in Quebecois church planters, describing them as "some of the most humble, coachable men I've met." Woody speaks French fluently and is a seasoned missionary. Language and culture provide the most significant coaching challenges. Here are Woody's observations:

1. Every church planter should be coached in his heart language. A significant number of French Canadians are bilingual, while some speak French only. But for coaching to be effective, being coached in the French language is important.

2. Coaching must be culturally relevant. Quebec has a unique religious, social, and emotional culture. Coaches who miss the culture will not help the church planter move closer to accomplishing his God-given vision.

Woody and Brian's perspectives do not bridge the cultural coaching gap with Hispanics or Canadians, but they fuel the conversation. Remember, to change the coaching culture, the conversation must change. To dismiss other cultures because of their complexities is not an option. Every church planter needs a coach. And every coaching relationship has unique cultural challenges to overcome.

Collect Coaching Stories

Don't define coaching, communicate for a season, and then never talk about it again. Over communicate in every written and spoken channel. Tell stories that affirm coaches and inspire planters. Let planters give short endorsements, similar to those on the back of books. You see an example at the end of every chapter in *Sending Well*. But here is another one:

My coach helped me by walking me through the painful days of church planting. We went through some serious lows during our first year as well as some incredible mountaintop highs. Having a coach by my side was critical in helping me keep a balanced and healthy perspective in every situation we encountered. I can't imagine having gone through our first year of church planting without my coach.

Jason Lamb
The Rising
Leesburg, Virginia
www.therising.cc

Know Your Why

A tidal wave of honor, respect, and support should greet church planting families as they start their journey. Our coaching structure should be fueled by an ethic of treating our gospel partners well. But with the best intentions, we often design next steps and productive behaviors in our heads, not our hearts. A compelling belief must fuel coaching as something bigger than coaching.

> As partners in the gospel, we say to church planters: We want you to succeed at what the King has assigned you to do.

Simon Sinek wrote the popular business book, *Begin with the Why: How Great Leaders Inspire Everyone to Take Action.* His simple explanation of how we influence people is noteworthy:

People don't buy what you do, they buy why you do it.[2]

Everything we do is built on the belief that no planter should plant alone. We are bound by a biblical ethic to love, support, and equip those families God sends. We abide with them through the wins and losses of church planting. Together, as partners in the gospel, we say to church planters: We want you to succeed at what the King has assigned you to do.

Affirmation and celebration are offered when planters lead well. Grace and comfort are extended when they don't. One platform to offer our love and support is great coaching. We want our coaching to be a vehicle to help planters pursue their unique kingdom assignment. We want to be great coaches. All of this is part of our common purpose to "Seek first the kingdom of God and his righteousness" (Matt. 6:33).

We decided to focus more on our why, stop being coaching apologists, and let God work through the process. This heart shift has positively affected our coaching culture. Your coaching culture is fueled by the "Why" of your coaches.

Lead coaches through a clarification process to change the conversation. Start the process by asking questions like, "What do you believe about the kingdom?" and "What do you believe about the church?" End with, "How does coaching undergird what you believe?"

Create a "We" Culture

Frankenmuth, Michigan, was an impressive venue for a meeting with church planting leadership in 2013. Settled by German immigrants in the mid-1800s, Frankenmuth is visited by millions of tourists each year. We gathered at the Bavarian Inn to discuss the future of church planter coaching in Michigan.

> How will we know when our coaching is working?

One of my favorite questions starts with "What is your biggest question about . . . ?" I love the clarity it brings to leaders about what's most important about a particular subject. I use this question often:

What is your biggest question about coaching?

Here is the exercise I used with the Michigan leaders:

- Write your biggest question about coaching on a card.
- Share your biggest question with a smaller group.

- Groups decide on one best question and transfer it to a wall poster.
- Groups rotate through questions to answer everyone's biggest questions.

The outcome of this exercise is to help groups experience working together to solve coaching challenges. Although they may struggle answering coaching questions, they are better equipped to solve local coaching challenges than "experts" from the outside.

The defining moment of the exercise came when we stood in a circle to debrief after everyone had rotated through the posters. One leader responded with emotion: *We can do this!* The shift came quickly from "Me" the coach, to "We" the coaches. A strong group prayer time followed. What was more memorable than the beautiful, snowy German village was God at work in the hearts of leaders who owned the challenge of coaching delivery.

Coaching has too many moving parts to run well all by itself. People are messy—including coaches and planters. Life is hectic, and we live every day like we are free-falling from an airplane. Ownership is vital to a healthy coaching culture.

Sending well is a team sport, not a solo activity. Our city visits helped foster a coaching culture within the greater kingdom community. How does a healthy coaching culture look? Everyone engaged in church planting understands and values church planter coaching. That must be our goal.

Our coaching results and momentum are better than ever. Local leaders own the vision to deliver great coaching to every church planter. But creating culture takes time and persistence.

Be Tenacious about Great Coaching

Changing the conversation and creating local coaching ownership affects

> Everyone engaged in church planting understands and values church planter coaching. That must be our goal.

coaching culture. But bad coaching kills coaching culture, no matter your momentum. Be tenacious about great coaching! When I think of the word *tenacious*, I think of my dog guarding his bone. Don't give up, and keep a grip on coaching quality. As your culture starts changing and growing, this will be your greatest challenge.

Never assume bad coaching always comes from bad coaches. If your leadership default is to blame the coaches, then your system will eventually die. Don't fire your coaches. Give them a chance at first. Create a culture that helps coaches succeed.

Critical quality control questions will build a great coaching culture:

- How do we set our coaches up for success?
- How are we training and resourcing active coaches?
- How accountable are coaches to follow the coaching process?
- How often do we communicate?
- How do we communicate the value of coaching to church planters?
- What kind of reporting do we expect?
- What does the coaching developmental plan process look like for active coaches?
- How do we celebrate and affirm coaches who advance their skills?
- How do we collect coaching feedback from coached planters?
- How does our system accommodate changing or releasing coaches if necessary?

Eight Characteristics of Bad Coaching

Be aware of how bad coaching looks. Below are eight characteristics of bad coaching:

1. A lack of credibility or capacity. Some of the best potential coaches have a high level of credibility among new planters but may not have the capacity to coach. And some who have the capacity to coach may not have the leadership credibility or experience needed to coach. Both capacity and credibility are needed for coaching fruitfulness.

2. An unclear purpose for coaching. Mentoring, advice-giving, counseling, and teaching are critical needs for church planters—but a coach's role is different. As coaching is clearly defined, the other voices become more effective and increase in value.

3. An unprepared coach. Coaching conversations are scheduled in advance. A high level of commitment to keep appointments is critical for both the coach and the planter. Great coaches schedule prep time before they coach.

4. Random coaching conversations. Although church planters receive valuable encouragement and advice in random ways, they need more. Our coaching metric is one conversation, every other week, for three to four months. Minimally, coaching needs to happen once a month. Coaching rhythm produces greater focus, efficient time management, and more accountability for follow-through.

5. Coaching conversations that don't end with action. Coaches help turn truth into action. If action isn't the result of a coaching conversation, it's not coaching at all. Move toward action by asking good questions.

6. No coaching agreement. Before coaching starts, a coach should verbally present a clear blueprint for how the coaching relationship works. Both parties should fully commit to the coaching process. An example of a coaching agreement is in Appendix G.

7. A poor handoff. Church planters have perfectly good reasons to be guarded and even skeptical when their new coach first approaches them. Coaches also feel awkward making a cold call introduction to their assigned planter. Could you imagine this call?

"Guess what? I'm your new coach. Coaching is going to be great because I'm an awesome coach. Now, get out your calendar, and let's schedule our next eight coaching conversations!"

To avoid these awkward handoffs, other coaches or church planting leaders should broker the new coaching relationship.

8. Assuming God's activity. God does not use tools; He uses people. Coaching isn't magic; it's merely a method to accomplish biblical results. Prayer, reviewing Scripture, and asking questions from a biblical angle are all crucial parts of great coaching.

Paul, the CEO of the Christian Movement

Paul and Barnabas launched into the apostolic blue ocean from a local church in Antioch. From humble beginnings, Paul became the human instrument for God's gospel expansion plan throughout the known world. In Paul, we see human qualities that God used to accomplish His purposes as well.

The work of God deep inside him produced strong, passionate appeals to his "partners in the gospel." One example is seen in Philippians 1:3–8. He valued them as people whom God deeply loved. The very character of God was embedded in Paul's newborn soul.

> *I thank my God in all my remembrance of you,* always in every prayer of mine for you all making my prayer with joy, because of your partnership in the gospel from the first day until now. And *I am sure of this,* that he who began a good work in you will bring it to completion at the day of Jesus Christ. It is right for me to feel this way about you all, because *I hold you in my heart,* for you are all partakers with me of grace, both in my imprisonment and in the defense and confirmation of the gospel. For God is my witness, how *I yearn for you all with the affection of Christ Jesus.* (Phil. 1:3–8, emphasis mine)

You feel the passion and emotion he felt toward his gospel partners through his strong statements of support. May God cultivate the same fire within our souls to care for our gospel partners.

The pursuit of a relationship is part of a Christian ethic, not merely a coaching standard. How much more, then, should coaches pursue those God has entrusted to them? Every church planting family needs to reminded:

God's got your back!

Joshua Whetstine is the Send Missionary and Coaching Champion in the Twin Cities. He described the responsibility of a coach when he said, "The coach must pursue the coached." This is Christlike and provides a picture of the gospel. Since God pursued us in Christ, we will pursue others.

Be Coached . . .

1. What part of your current coaching culture can you celebrate?

2. What steps can you take to build a stronger coaching culture?

3. Whom can you trust to help own church planter coaching?

4. What planting family needs special attention from you now?

My Coach Helps . . .

My coach helps me maintain perspective. While he listens to what's going on, his questioning and guidance help reshift my focus to where it needs to be to continue to be effective. Ministry has proven to be incredibly lonely. Often we're not sure whom we can trust and open up to. My coach has provided a safe place to let my guard down and speak freely to navigate through each season.

Bryan Ball
Storytellers Church
Chesterfield, Michigan
www.storytellersmi.org

 **CHAPTER 18**

Practice Church Planter Coaching

In 2016, Allen Iverson received the highest honor a National Basketball Association (NBA) player could receive. Iverson was elected to the NBA Hall of Flame. Only the elite, best of the best superstars belong in this exclusive club. Since the creation of the Hall in 1959, only 180 players have been elected to date.

Iverson's nickname, "The Answer," was backed by his amazing ability to outplay his opponents. Called "one of the most lethal scorers in NBA history," he scored more than twenty-four thousand points in his seventeen-year career, most of which was played with the Philadelphia 76ers.[1]

Beyond the basketball court, Allen Iverson left a lasting impression as well. His rant about "practice" in a 2002 press conference is more famous for some than his Hall of Fame or basketball court accomplishments.

Iverson was born with rare natural basketball talent. No question, practice was not as necessary for him as it was for others. Frustrated by the media's skepticism of his practice habits, Iverson made his famous statement, "talking about practice." Over the course of two minutes, he repeated the word "practice" twenty-four times. Iverson made his case that playing the game was more important than practice.[2]

Great coaches love to coach. However, the skill of coaching church planters is different from basketball talent. Coaching is the most unnatural skill you will ever attempt to master. The core of coaching goes against every human instinct. To learn a new approach to discipleship and leadership development takes practice. The raw material that makes a great coach starts with a heart for God and love for people. But a coach's skill develops over time through repetition or practice. A strong coaching culture reproduces coachable planters and great coaches.

The "Me" to "We" Shift

Coaching planters is a team sport, particularly if your vision is to deliver great coaching to every church planter. When you include the most important member of the church planting core group, the church planting wife, then the need escalates. Then consider the racial, ethnic, cultural, and generational diversity among planters. No matter their skill level, a few coaches cannot possibly meet the need both in quantity and quality.

> A pod is a family of coaches who love their city and the planters who live there.

We call our coaching groups in cities "Coaching Pods." A pod is a family of coaches who love their city and the planters who live there. Although this is a book about coaching, this family of coaches sees the King's glory and the King's message as the reasons for their existence.

These coaches are obsessed with sending missionaries into their city to plant churches. But they are equally obsessed with sending them loved, encouraged, prepared, and supported.

So, what are their habits, impulses, and instincts? You will discover five practices of great church planter coaches in this chapter. The list is not inclusive, but it details the five we believe are the best of the best practices for us. To create a strong coaching system, choosing the narrative is critical.

Practice. We are talking about practice. Church planter coaching gets better through coaching repetitions: learning from coaches, mastering the basics, establishing metrics, peer coaching, and multiplying coaches.

Like the five principles in chapter 4, these five practices were chosen to keep coaching simple and keep coaches coaching. In the end, we want to take coaching from a "Me" to "We" focus. These five practices will help us get there. How does a family of coaches, or "coaching pod," work together to grow as coaches and serve planters?

> *Church planter coaching gets better through coaching repetitions.*

Five Practices of Great Church Planter Coaching Pods

Practice 1: Learn to coach from coaches.

The best way to learn to coach is to coach and be coached. Coaches learn from each other. A strong coaching culture involves more than a few well-trained people who coach and promote coaching. And coach training events do not necessarily build a coaching culture, no matter how good the events might be.

Active coaches are the foundation of a strong coaching culture. The practices of church planter coaching are ongoing behaviors that help coaches improve their skills. As church planter coaches improve their skills, the leaders they coach reap the benefits.

I have learned more being coached by great coaches than I've learned from books, resources, or training. My relationships with those coaches have been invaluable. And strong coaches have motivated me to want to learn and grow.

If you want to grow as a coach, then find other coaches and be with them:

- **Ask them questions about what they do.** Prepare your questions for them in advance. Ask them how they got started, how they were trained, and who has coached them. Ask them for advice on how to be a better coach.

- **Watch them work.** In some cases, coaches may allow you to sit in on one of their coaching sessions if they have a willing coaching client. I have trained coaches with this method and have found it to be a great way to help.
- **Ask them to be your coach.** As you grow from being coached, God will show you how you can help others, including the people you coach.

> *Knowledge of the coaching disciplines is important, but until you coach people, a credential, certificate, or title is meaningless.*

Knowledge of the coaching discipline is important, but until you coach people, a credential, certificate, or title is meaningless. As Keith Webb said, ". . . coaching is not about certificates—it's about being helpful to others."[3]

Practice 2: Master the coaching basics.

Though many church planters are already active in small groups, accountability groups, vision/planning teams, and more, coaching is another way to offer community to planters by drawing out what God is doing in their lives.

What makes a new coach ready to coach church planters in the context of community? Practicing the fundamentals of coaching, which are simple: listen, care, and encourage.

Listen. Church planter coaching thrives on a relational connection between two disciples—a connection that's cultivated within a great listening environment. Here are five ways to create that kind of environment:

1. **Great questions.** Use easy questions to get the conversation going. Listen carefully, and your church planter will give you the next questions!
2. **Advanced preparation.** Email five to ten coaching questions two days before the coaching conversation and ask for

the answers to be returned before your meeting. This will help begin the conversation and maximize your listening time.

3. **Comfortable setting.** Coaching in the car or a crowded coffee shop isn't ideal. Be somewhere you can be all there, and use a reliable phone and Internet connection.

4. **Practical tools.** A headset, a note-taking method, and a quiet location all help keep a listening focus.

5. **Email follow-up.** Use this to compare notes, reinforce action steps, and listen even further to the church planter you are coaching.

Great coaches are great listeners. Anyone can interrogate and manipulate, and anyone can ask questions or complete forms. But a great coach listens to learn. And a great coach listens to the heart. The bottom line? A great church planter coach loves to listen!

Care. Church planters can feel like they are vending machines, ready to dispense what those around them need. Planters are approached by people who expect to get what they want—and quickly. This dynamic added to the fear of disappointing people can cause church planters to strive harder—and quite possibly to feel that nobody cares for them. Also, they develop reasons not to care for themselves. The most obvious reason (at least they think) is that they don't have that luxury.

To help care for church planters, coaches embrace the core practices of serving and giving.

> For you have been called to live in freedom, my brothers and sisters. But don't use your freedom to satisfy your sinful nature. Instead, use your freedom to serve one another in love. (Gal. 5:13 NLT)

Encourage. One of the most important attributes of a church planter is courage. The planters you coach will either be encouraged or discouraged on some level. To be discouraged means to be deprived of courage, hope, or confidence. The Latin prefix *dis* means to go in reverse or in a negative direction.

To be encouraged, on the other hand, means to be inspired with courage, spirit, or confidence, or to be stimulated by assistance. The prefix *en* means to cause a person to be in a place. Coaches can make a difference by helping a planter move to a place of greater courage.

One way to encourage through coaching is to help the church planters you coach celebrate wins. Leaders spend much of their time "putting out fires" as opposed to being proactive and running after God-given passions.

Help the planters you coach discover what is right in their world. Speak openly about the things you see them doing well (even small things) and the progress they are making toward their goals. Look for God's work in their lives and point it out. A great church planter coach encourages!

Church planter coaches develop through mastering the basics: listen, care, and encourage.

Practice 3: Establish coaching metrics.

Coaching is simple—but as we've said, it's not easy. A formal coaching role may not be suitable for everyone. Other mission-critical roles like counselor, advisor, teacher, and mentor are needed on the sending team in your city.

We champion the idea that the best coaching is coaching that happens. We also face a challenge in this—how do we get better at the coaching that is already happening?

Being a great coach involves having consistent one-on-one conversations with people and asking lots of questions. But questions and consistency can still result in bad coaching—we must be intentional about our growth as coaches.

If you are serious about being a church planter coach, you must also be serious about great coaching. What is your growth plan as a church planter coach? How do you know your coaching is working?

Coaching metrics are important. Here are some simple ways to measure how you are doing as a coach:

1. **Ask the person you are coaching.** "How can I be a better coach for you?" The planter you coach may not answer the first time you ask, but keep asking.
2. **Measure the number of new steps.** Each time you coach, count how many specific actions are planned and executed.
3. **Assess how much you are talking.** If you are talking more than 20 percent of the time in a coaching conversation, then your coaching is marginalized. Your goal is to help church planters process by listening and asking.
4. **Count the number of conversations.** The value of coaching rises in proportion to how much and how often you meet. The best coaching happens on a schedule—every other week for three to four months. When a regular schedule is followed, accountability for follow-through is higher, and one conversation builds on another.
5. **Measure the effort.** The best coaching features a coaching guide (agenda) sent from the coach two days in advance. This agenda is completed by the person being coached and returned to the coach one day before the coaching conversation. The coach then spends a few minutes preparing for the meeting by thinking about deeper questions.

As you engage church planters through coaching conversations, where should you focus to get better at coaching? Great church planter coaching comes from utilizing coaching metrics and committing to grow as a coach.

Practice 4: Coach a peer.

Mark Clifton, Send Network Senior Director of Replant, wrote, "Discipleship isn't something you learn in a class or at a conference. Discipleship happens as you become who you hang out with."[4]

Peer coaches disciple each other through ongoing coaching conversations. One of the best benefits of peer coaching is that it keeps coaches coaching. Coaches who coach are more likely to grow than coaches who only attend training.

Essentials of Trip Planning. My family took one vacation each year when I was growing up. Every summer for twelve years, we drove from northeast Tennessee to Vineland, New Jersey. Before the days of the smartphone with GPS, all we had to guide us was a folding paper map. The unfolding and refolding of this paper map was quite a task. Normally the maps were so big that, in a real crisis, you had to stop the car and open the map on the hood. The more my parents studied the map before we left home, the more likely we would make it to Vineland without stress. Where do we want to go? How are we going to get there? Where will we stop along the way? Looking at the map only after we left home was a sure recipe for disaster.

When launching a church planter coaching initiative in your city, early momentum is key. Just as in our trips to New Jersey for twelve straight summers, starting well is crucial. Answering simple questions like: "Where are we going?" and "How are we going to get there?" is vital.

Keep Training in Perspective. Training is a good place to start but seldom establishes long-term momentum. Common language, principles, and practices are products of strong coach training. However, busy leaders are constantly in and out of quality training events over the life of their ministries. Therefore, training is not a great destination, but it can help in planning the trip.

Keith Webb determined that training that required immediate follow-up was proven to be 300-percent more effective than training experiences that required no follow-up. Coaching following any training is worth the investment of time.[5]

Peer coaching puts coaches to work immediately and establishes the momentum needed to build a church planter coaching culture. The goal is to get coaches coaching and then keep them coaching.

The coaching platform provides a practical way to deal with the demands of ministry and develop a new skill simultaneously.

Ready to Travel. Our one-day coach orientation looks like training to the naked eye. But we provide the "trip orientation" for church planter coaching. Imagine key coaching leaders and new coaches standing together in a room, looking at a map and planning a road trip. Incidentally, we call our one-day coach orientation the *One Day Coaching Map.*

> *Peer coaching puts coaches to work immediately and establishes the momentum needed to build a church planter coaching culture.*

The value of the Map lies in the peer coaching relationships formed that continue for at least eight weeks afterward. Coaching momentum and culture begin immediately. Like freshman orientation in college, relationships begin at the Map that may last for years to come.

Cities that have hosted a One Day Coaching Map resulting in strong peer coaching relationships have the best chance of establishing a solid church planter coaching system. Peer coaching is a crucial part of the process. Our internal coaching scorecard includes the percentage of Map attendees who engage in peer coaching conversations after the Map.

Here are three reasons why I love peer coaching:

1. If you have a peer, you have a free coach.
2. The best way to learn to coach is by coaching and being coached.
3. God does amazing things when two disciples walk together.

You can begin peer coaching today, no matter your coach training experience. All you need is a peer who wants to grow as a coach and a leader. Who can be your peer coach? When can you start?

Practice 5: Multiply coaches.

People don't fit well into formulas. We live in a healthy tension between worlds such as organic versus intentional, or God's part versus our part. Much to my disappointment as I've dialogued with leaders all over North America, I have never found a comfortable, formula-driven answer.

The best we have are our experiences plus biblical examples of reproduction applied to our current situations. We are inspired by examples like T4T (*T4T: A Discipleship Re-revolution* by Steve Smith and Ying Kai) and David Garrison's book on movements (*Church Planting Movements: How God Is Redeeming a Lost World*). These discussions give us hope that the best is yet to come.

Hope exists because of the unlimited supply of God's power and favor. The book of Acts is a historical rendering of the way God moves. Paul gave the theological foundation for what was demonstrated in Acts: "Now to him who is able to do far more abundantly than all that we ask or think, according to the power at work within us" (Eph. 3:20).

We can contribute space for God to work by creating multiplying environments. That's our part. The results are His part. Paul's words in 1 Corinthians illustrate the closest we get to a multiplication formula in the Bible: "I planted, Apollos watered, but God gave the growth" (1 Cor. 3:6).

Church planter coaches have a unique role in the spiritual journeys of the planters they coach. When God develops one of His followers in community, part of their leadership story includes ongoing, personal, one-on-one conversations.

I want to multiply church planter coaches because every church planter needs one. Every church planting wife needs one as well. Planters and their wives are racially, ethnically, culturally, and generationally diverse. Below is a short exercise to help you find church planter coaches.

Who are your next church planter coaches?

- Church planters
- Church planting wives
- Church planting team members
- Professional coaches in newer churches
- Pastors/staff who have planted
- Pastors/staff or members who are highly engaged in sending churches
- Who else?

Create a list of five potential church planter coaches in your region. Email an interesting article about coaching to those people and tell them what you are thinking. Look for opportunities to develop and launch new church planter coaches in your church and city.

The Coaching Burden

Unfortunately, not all coaching is great, and not all coaches are properly motivated. As church planter coaches, we must carry the burden to make coaching great. Becoming a great church planter coach involves more than skill development.

Sending well through coaching is ultimately about our integrity as coaches. Will we let Christ continue to work in us? Or will we attempt to coach in our own strength while we're still settled deep in our personal ruts? Coaching from the latter position perpetuates a false sense of self-importance—and doesn't lay the groundwork for the results we want in the lives of church planters.

We want to multiply coaches in order to multiply coaching and guarantee that every church planter in North America has a coach. We want to coach well. And we want to live well in order to coach well.

Proverbs 4:23–26 addresses the challenge of self-leadership that should be the practice of a great coach:

Keep your heart with all vigilance, for from it flow the springs of life. Put away from you crooked speech, and put devious talk far from you. Let your eyes look directly forward, and your gaze be straight before you. Ponder the path of your feet; then all your ways will be sure.

Be Coached . . .

1. What practice is most important to you?

2. What practice would you add?

3. What practice is most relevant to your personal coaching now?

4. What step will you take to upgrade your coaching as a result?

My Coach Helps . . .

My coach helps me think through different situations and scenarios to see all sides and make informed decisions. It has been a blessing to have someone who understands and allows me to make mistakes but offers guidance to correct or avoid them. Also, having a voice that I trust who has been there and also has seen the other side of ministry is an invaluable resource.

Nick Erickson
Redemption Church
Ogden, Utah
www.redemptionutah.com

Frequently Asked Questions

Capture the questions that planters, coaches, and church planting leaders ask and craft your answers. One way we have done that in the past is to ask groups, "What is your biggest question about coaching?"

The health of your coaching system is at stake as you design clear, intentional answers. And the greatest value of a FAQ list is that everyone in your coaching system will be on the same page.

Below are eight examples. Be inspired by the list, but resist the temptation to copy the answers—they are likely to be different anyway. The point is not that you have to answer them our way, but that you have to answer them.

Create your FAQ list. Gather a group of your coaches and leaders in a room or on a video conference call and answer their questions in your own words. Let an editor clean them up—your answer will be easier to remember and more authentic to those who ask them.

The process of writing answers will have a unifying effect on those involved, and your coaches and coaching leaders will be one step closer to moving from "Me" (I coach church planters) to "We" (We coach church planters). Your coaching culture will grow stronger as a result of this process.

What is the difference between coaching and mentoring?

A coach draws out; a mentor pours in. A coach is assigned for a season and provides a support role. A mentor offers a longer-term relationship and draws from his experience and expertise to provide what is needed. Both roles are critical in the life of a church planter. Ideally, those roles are best coming from different relationships.

How do I know my coaching is working?

The vision is to deliver great coaching to every church planter. The first step is to understand that each coaching relationship is unique. Coaches must be passionate about providing the best possible coaching for each planter. Our one-day coach orientation includes a discussion of coaching metrics that help local coaches clearly define how they will measure coaching success. This question is answered in greater detail on pages 240–241.

How does successful coaching look?

Two basic indicators of successful coaching are measured through these questions: *How often do the coach and the planter meet? How many times do the coach and the planter meet?* The frequency of meetings and number of meetings are proven metrics of great coaching. Great coaching is one ongoing conversation between a coach and church planter with multiple installments. Coaching includes continuing where the last conversation ended and is a vehicle that moves planters to the next stop. More coaching metrics are needed and should be established locally.

How many planters can someone coach at one time?

Although there are exceptions, the Send Network Coaching Team recommends one planter per coach, particularly in the beginning phases of your coaching system.

How long does a coaching relationship last?

A typical coaching relationship lasts for one to two years and consists of twelve to sixteen coaching conversations per year.

What if a planter does not want to be coached?

Creating a pod of coaches who are 100-percent committed to great coaching raises the coachability among planters. But great coaching requires a 100-percent commitment from the church planter as well. Communicating coaching stories, providing a diverse coaching pool, and challenging coaches to grow are all parts of our strategy for making coaching worth the investment.

What is the difference between coaching and discipleship?

Coaching is an important element of discipleship that focuses on accountability, hearing God, and obedience. Other crucial elements of discipleship include (but are not limited to) teaching, mentoring, advising, and counseling.

Should a church planter coach ever give advice?

We encourage coaches to develop asking and listening skills that give a church planter space to process all the directive voices in his life. God may lead coaches to warn, encourage, and advise by speaking into the situation. However, those functions are not the primary role of a church planter coach. Church planting catalysts, sending-church pastors, trainers, and seasoned church planters provide valuable directive voices in the process.

Great Coaching Development Guide

Serving: *I enjoy helping others succeed in life and ministry.*
- ❏ I connect with planters I coach between coaching conversations.
- ❏ I ask how I can improve my coaching.
- ❏ I send follow-up emails after our meetings with action items and highlights.
- ❏ I calendar multiple coaching meetings in advance.
- ❏ I plan twenty minutes before and after a coaching call for prep, prayer, review, and evaluation.

Goal:

Actions:

Believing: *I am confident in God's ability to transform people.*
- ❏ I experience the transforming power of Christ in my life.
- ❏ I ask transformational questions.
- ❏ I coach the planter, not the plant.
- ❏ I coach beyond symptoms to heart issues.
- ❏ I view the planter through a biblical lens.

Goal:

Actions:

Listening: *I give the gift of listening.*
- ❑ I coach in a listening environment free from distractions.
- ❑ I summarize back what I hear planters saying.
- ❑ I ask follow-up questions based on the previous answers.
- ❑ I take notes during my coaching conversations.
- ❑ I talk no more than 20 percent of the time.

Goal:

Actions:

Cheering: *I celebrate wins, both large and small.*
- ❑ I use social media to cheer for the planters I coach.
- ❑ I affirm the activity of God in the planter's life and ministry.
- ❑ I visit the websites of the planters I coach.
- ❑ I affirm strengths, gifts, and experiences.
- ❑ I celebrate completed goals and accomplished action steps.

Goal:

Actions:

Praying: *I embrace the Holy Spirit's work in the life and ministry of a leader.*
- ❑ I pray with and for planters I coach.
- ❑ I ask planters to pray for me including specific requests.
- ❑ I help the people I coach recognize the Holy Spirit's work in their lives.

❑ I reference Scripture when coaching.
❑ I prompt planters to cultivate intercessory prayer teams.

Goal:

Actions:

Pressing: *I understand the next step is the most important one.*

❑ I help the planters I coach create SMART goals.
❑ I ask planters to calendar deadlines for their action items.
❑ I send coaching guides in advance of coaching conversations.
❑ I expect coaching guides to be completed and returned in advance of coaching.
❑ I ask strong follow-up questions to help planters create action items.

Goal:

Actions:

Supporting: *I believe there's no one-size-fits-all formula for success.*

❑ I avoid giving advice.
❑ I help clarify the planter's desired outcomes for the coaching conversation.
❑ I keep planters focused on their stated goals and outcomes.
❑ I help planters brainstorm multiple options to provide strategic solutions.
❑ I ask for personal highlights at the end of each coaching conversation.

Goal:

Actions:

Relating: *I engage coaching relationships with patience and persistence.*

- ☐ I use notes from previous coaching conversations to help me prepare to coach.
- ☐ I begin each coaching conversation by making personal, informal connections.
- ☐ I begin my coaching meetings on time.
- ☐ I end my coaching meetings on time.
- ☐ I discuss a coaching agreement at the beginning of each relationship.

Goal:

Actions:

Growing: *My goal is to become a great coach.*

- ☐ I ask open-ended questions.
- ☐ I know the names of the spouse and children of every planter I coach.
- ☐ I evaluate my coaching after every conversation.
- ☐ I keep the planter accountable through honest conversations.
- ☐ I have an ongoing development plan for my coaching skills.

Goal:

Actions:

Planting: *I help church planters pursue their unique kingdom assignment.*

- ☐ I ask questions aimed toward specific church planting outcomes.
- ☐ I coach toward development needs that surfaced during the assessment process.

❑ I coach the planter back to previous principles learned during training.

❑ I ask questions aimed toward specific church planting behaviors.

❑ I keep current with planting practices by reading blogs, books, etc.

Goal:

Actions:

Multiply Coaches for the Mission

When Jesus said, "Therefore, pray to the Lord of the harvest to send out workers into His harvest" (Matt. 9:38 HCSB), He invited us to be part of the sending as well as the harvesting.

The **One-Day Coaching Map** is a simple workshop that will sharpen your coaching skills and help multiply church planter coaches. You will learn to expand your personal sending capacity through ongoing coaching relationships with church planters.

The following four experiences will accelerate your development as a church planter coach:

One-Day Coaching Map: Help launch a coaching team to provide high-quality church planter coaching.

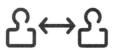

Peer Coaching: Coach and be coached with a peer by phone or video conferencing in preparation for church planter coaching.

 **Church Planter Coaching:** Coach one church planter by phone or video conferencing twice a month for up to four months, twice a year.

 **Coaching Pod:** Become part of a coaching team that provides quality church planter coaches and coaching for your region on an ongoing basis.

 **APPENDIX D**

Church Planter Coaching 360

Assess the Need

How many planters under two years' post launch
need coaches? _____

How many planter deployments do you anticipate
in the next twelve months? _____

Total coaching relationships needed over the next
twelve months: _____

Measure the Capacity

How many competent and credible coaches do you
have? _____

How many church planter coaches are actively
coaching church planters? _____

Total number of new coaches needed to meet demand: _____

We have a delivery system for the orientation of new
coaches. Yes No

Examine the Quality

Coaching conversations have predetermined agendas. Yes No

The number of coaching meetings is prescribed. Yes No

The number of coaching meetings is reported. Yes No

We have a development plan for our current coaches. Yes No

Next steps to upgrade the quality of our church planter coaching system:

Goal: Date:
Goal: Date:
Goal: Date:
Goal: Date:

Your Top Five Church Planter Coaches:

1.   Email:
2.   Email:
3.   Email:
4.   Email:
5.   Email:

Notes:

 **APPENDIX E**

Two Equipping Paths to Help Mobilize Sending Churches

The North American Mission Board (NAMB) offers resources to help mobilize and equip sending churches. Below are examples:

Sending Church Labs—A twenty-four-hour equipping workshop for churches interested in upgrading their sending efforts. Best practices from current sending churches, tools, resources, and stories from current sending pastors are part of the agenda.

Catch the Vision Tours—A two-day experience in a city to help a church find a church planter to join as a supporting or sending church partner. Local church planters and missionary leaders orient leaders from other cities with the local culture, challenges, and opportunities.

More sending church free resources are found at https://www.namb.net/church-mobilization/church-mobilization-resources. Information like: *10 Ways to Care for a Planter* and *Sending Church Expectations* are among a collection of best practices to move sending to a new level.

Another valuable sending church resource is Pat Hood's book, *The Sending Church: The Church Must Leave the Building*. God's amazing missionary revolution at LifePoint Church in Smyrna, Tennessee, is a must-read.

Pat tells the story of his personal and church transitions that moved LifePoint from a good church to a surrendered church. Churches around you, including yours, will not necessarily become LifePoint. God's story will be unique. But the potential of what God can do through your church as a sending church is encouraging.

LifePoint Church (www.lifepointchurch.org/livesent) has sent staff members and leaders locally and as far away as Bangkok and Brussels. Pat describes their newly discovered priority of sending:

> We have challenged our people to engage and embrace the mission of God through tithing, giving generously above the tithe, and going. This is not a business; it's a battle! And people who attend LifePoint are not customers or even just members, they're missionaries.[1]

Expectations Worksheet for Planters[1]

Clint Clifton, Send City Missionary, Washington, D.C. Church Planter, Pillar Church, Dumfries, VA Used by Permission

Every new church planter has expectations about how things will turn out in the early stages of church planting, but not all expectations will become reality. How well a church planter manages his expectations will contribute a great deal to his sense of personal effectiveness in ministry.

Just this week, I met with two new church planters and I asked them both the same question. "If I could somehow look into the future and I tell you that one year from now your church would have an average of seventy-five in attendance each week, how would that make you feel?" The first church planter responded positively by saying, "I'd be amazed that seventy-five people would come to hear me preach." The other one honestly confessed, "I'd quit." You see the only difference between these two guys is their expectations. If they both had the exact same experience, one would finish the year ready to give up and the other would be encouraged.

Knowing this, I'd like to challenge you to spend some time exploring your expectations for the first year of ministry. Below is a list of questions that will help to reveal your expectations. After you understand your expectations, you can begin to consider how you will respond if and when your expectations are exceeded or unrealized.

The wise church planter will remember the Scripture's warnings concerning the accomplishment of our plans and will evaluate his success not on his own accomplishments but on the promised guidance provided by our Savior day to day.

> Many are the plans in a person's heart, but it is the LORD's purpose that prevails. (Prov. 19:21 NIV)

> The heart of man plans his way, but the LORD establishes his steps. (Prov. 16:9 ESV)

> "I am with you always, even until the end of the age." (Matt. 28:20 NLT)

Review the following list of expectations, marking the ones you expect will be true after your first year of public worship services.

EXPECTATION	REALITY	
❏	❏	My family will settle into a "normal" rhythm to our life and ministry.
❏	❏	I will enjoy the work.
❏	❏	My family will be settled into a stable housing and school situation.
❏	❏	The church will have a strong, committed base of at least ten families.
❏	❏	We will have other significant ministry partners serving with us.
❏	❏	The church will have held its first baptism service.

EXPECTATION	REALITY	
❏	❏	The church will have a stable meeting location.
❏	❏	The church will average more than one hundred people in weekly worship services.
❏	❏	The church will have a quality worship leader.
❏	❏	The church will have affirmed at least one other elder.
❏	❏	Our church constitution will be written and agreed upon.
❏	❏	The church will have deacons.
❏	❏	The church will have members.
❏	❏	The church will have a membership course.
❏	❏	The church will have given monetary support to another planting or revitalization project.
❏	❏	The church will have identified and helped to prepare another church planter.
❏	❏	The church will have organized and participated in a foreign mission trip.
❏	❏	Our worship services could be described as joyful and spiritually meaningful.
❏	❏	The leaders of each ministry are Spirit-filled, obedient Christians.
❏	❏	The men and women who serve closest to me in the work respect my leadership.
❏	❏	The men and women who serve closest to me in the work respect my walk with God.
❏	❏	The men and women who serve closest to me in the work are my closest friends.
❏	❏	People who attend our church will invite others to attend regularly.

EXPECTATION	REALITY	
❏	❏	I will be able to see the result of my preaching in the lives of those who attend regularly.
❏	❏	I will have had a major conflict with a key member of the core team or staff.
❏	❏	I will have angered someone so much they left our church.
❏	❏	I will have a good relationship with the other church planters in my network.
❏	❏	I regularly help other church planters with advice or encouragement.
❏	❏	I will have at least one major regret concerning the way I've led so far.
❏	❏	I read and study regularly.
❏	❏	My prayer life is meaningful and frequent.
❏	❏	I am pastoral in my home with my wife and family.

Six-Month Coaching Check-in Using the Expectations Worksheet

- What is exceeding your expectations?
- What is exactly what you expected?
- What is below your expectations?
- How would your wife answer these three questions?
- What have you seen God do over the last six months?
- How can you celebrate?
- What adjustments are in order as a result of this conversation?

Sample Coaching Agreement

Coaching helps church planters pursue their unique kingdom assignment.

Focus Your Energy

Your initial coaching process includes eight coaching conversations over four months. You will identify key areas where you need to grow. Your coach will also help you establish goals, action plans, and time lines. Coaching focuses on the whole planter. Examples of growth areas include:

Personal
- Spiritual Heath
- Family Spiritual Heath
- Physical Health
- Family Physical Health
- Mental and Emotional Health

Planting
- Reaching New Believers
- Making Disciple Makers
- Multiplying Your Church
- Pursuing Sustainability

Lead from the Heart

The influence of coaching moves beyond simply leading successfully. Coaching provides an environment for God to work through personal growth and heart change.

Get Started!

Your coach will email an agenda for each meeting that includes a series of questions. This will remind you of your appointment and help you prepare. You set your agenda. What do you want to work on? What is God saying to you? Where do you need to grow? Complete the agenda twenty-four hours in advance and return to your coach.

Make a Commitment

The key for an effective coaching relationship is a 100-percent commitment by the coach and the church planter to the coaching process. Your coach is fully committed to helping you. He is a trained and experienced coach.

Core Coaching Commitments

- We will schedule appointments in advance and keep them.
- We will reschedule immediately in case of emergencies.
- We will have good Internet/computer access and coach in distraction-free environments.
- We will use coaching guides.
- We will follow through on goals and actions.
- We will pray for each other.
- We will be accountable to each other.
- We will keep the content of our conversations confidential.

_____

Coach   Date

_____

Church Planter   Date

Therefore, preparing your minds for action, and being sober-minded, set your hope fully on the grace that will be brought to you at the revelation of Jesus Christ. (1 Pet. 1:13)

 **APPENDIX H**

Great Coaching Checklist

Planter _____ Date _____

Did I ask about family members by name? _____ Yes _____ No

What significant details did you learn about his family today?

Did I help establish a clear objective? _____ Yes _____ No

What objective(s) did your planter work on today?

Did I press for action? _____ Yes _____ No

What steps did your planter create?

Did I ask great questions? _____ Yes _____ No

Example(s) of a great question I used:

What did I do well today?

What can I do better next time?

NOTES:

 **APPENDIX I**

Credibility and Capacity Checklist for Potential Coaches

This checklist helps create a coaching invite list. The purpose is to discover people who are more likely to coach planters successfully. Checking every box for an invitee is unlikely, but this should help you narrow the list. Getting the right people in the room is vital to long-term coaching results. Your checklist will be different, but the following provides a template you can use.

Credibility

- ☐ **Leads leaders:** Leaders come to him for advice and relationship.
- ☐ **Multiplies leaders:** Leaders move through his church on to other ministries, etc.
- ☐ **Experience in context:** Lives and ministers in the area where he is coaching.
- ☐ **Planted in context:** Has planted a church in the area where he is coaching.
- ☐ **Multiplies churches:** His church is engaged in church planting.
- ☐ **Planted successfully:** Has planted a church that has grown numerically and spiritually.
- ☐ **Coaching credentials:** Has been trained as a coach.
- ☐ **Growing:** Demonstrates a teachable spirit and passion for personal growth.

Capacity

- ❏ **Collaborative:** Works well with leaders and teams outside his church.
- ❏ **Shepherding:** Invests time and energy caring for leaders outside his church.
- ❏ **Available:** Invests time and energy in causes outside his church.
- ❏ **Mentoring:** Pours into others in one-on-one relationships.
- ❏ **Prompt:** Returns calls, emails, and texts.
- ❏ **Dependable:** Schedules and keeps appointments.
- ❏ **Flexible:** Open to different methodologies.
- ❏ **Attentive:** Listens closely to what others are saying.

Acknowledgments

"No one sits in the chair alone." I have no idea who deserves credit for those words, but I know I sit in a really big chair. God knew I needed lots of help. People like John Bailey, Jeff Christopherson, Artie Davis, Bill Howard, Ray Jones, Bob Logan, Neal McGlohon, Glenn Smith, Ed Stetzer, and many others who have walked beside me at critical junctures. "Iron sharpens iron" (Prov. 27:17). God has blessed and sharpened me by being next to people like these.

Jesus found me years ago when I was not looking for Him. His grace and mercy are confounding. Thank you, Jesus. May this book influence Your sending mission.

My biggest cheerleader on Earth was a cheerleader when I met her in college years ago. Thank you to my sweetheart, Yvette.

I am forever grateful for the platform and resources of the North American Mission Board. I am blessed to be on the team.

Sending Well would never have happened without the stamina, passion, and contributions of Olivia Gregory. Olivia is an incredible coach, writer, and editor who is family to us. Elijah Hieber created many of the illustrations in this book . . . and he is only eighteen years old! Elijah is a great young man with great potential. Eddie Hancock and Jamie Limato contributed to this project more than they know, including writing sections for me when I was out of time, energy, and ideas. Both of these men are incredible coaches and coach developers. They are friends, brothers, and gifts to the body of Christ.

273

Notes

Foreword

1. https://books.google.com/books?id=tvLgDAAAQBAJ&pg=PA1
12&lpg=PA112&dq="A+good+coach+can+change+a+game.+A+great+c
oach+can+change+a+life."+%20+John+Wooden&source=bl&ots=o06m-
W62Upu&sig=IZFkKMnxq67socoA2Jzfn40bxWk&hl=en&sa=X&v
ed=0ahUKEwj_p8Gi9JHWAhUT8mMKHXktCCcQ6AEIXTAN
#v=onepage&q="A%20good%20coach%20can%20change%20a%20
game.%20A%20great%20coach%20can%20change%20a%20life."%20
☒%20John%20Wooden&f=false

Part One

1. Artie Davis first introduced me to using the idea of the "How,"
"What," "Why," and "We" filters in 2012. Artie Davis, *Craveable: The
Irresistible Jesus in Me* (Lake Mary, FL: Passio, 2013).

Chapter 1

1. United States Olympic Committee, "History," 2017.
Accessed February 14, 2017, http://www.teamusa.org/
USA-Synchronized-Swimming/About-USA-Synchro/History.

2. Will Mancini, *Church Unique: How Missional Leaders Cast
Vision, Capture Culture, and Create Movement* (San Francisco, CA:
Jossey-Bass, 2008), 86.

3. Jeff Christopherson, *Kingdom Matrix: Designing a Church for
the Kingdom of God*, Expanded ed. (Boise, ID: Elevate Publishing,
2012), 56.

4. Jeff Christopherson and Mac Lake, *Kingdom First: Starting
Churches that Shape Movements* (Nashville, TN: B&H Publishing
Group, 2015), 210.

5. Clint Clifton, *Church Planting Thresholds: A Gospel-Centered Guide* (n.p.: New City Network, 2016), 151.

Chapter 2

1. "Chariots of Fire (1981)." Accessed January 28, 2017, http://www.imdb.com/title/tt0082158.

2. "Jerusalem" by William Blake, 1804. Accessed January 28, 2017, http://www.poetry-archive.com/b/jerusalem.html.

3. Jeff Christopherson and Mac Lake, *Kingdom First: Starting Churches that Shape Movements* (Nashville, TN: B&H Publishing Group, 2015), 40.

4. Mac Lake, "The Big Responsibility of Big Results," December 15, 2015. Accessed February 20, 2017, http://www.maclakeonline.com/leadership/the-big-responsibility-of-big-results/.

5. Peter Scazzero, "The Emotionally Healthy Church Planter," 2012. Accessed February 19, 2017, http://www.emotionallyhealthy.org/wp-content/uploads/2015/07/EHChurchPlanter.pdf.

6. See www.christianitytoday.com/edstetzer/.

7. See https://exponential.org/.

8. Ed Stetzer and Todd Wilson, "No Church Planting Family Alone: Leading Voices Weigh in on Top Challenges Facing Today's Church Planters." Accessed November 29, 2016, http://www.christianitytoday.com/assets/10182.pdf.

9. Ibid.

10. Ibid.

Chapter 3

1. Heather Bond, "5 Reasons Why I Want My Husband to Have a Coach: Coaching Reflections from a Church Planting Wife," *CNBC Horizon* 29, no. 3 (June 2016): 17.

2. Tony Stoltzfus, "What Makes a Coach?" 2006. Accessed February 28, 2017, http://coach22.com/discover-coaching/resources/what_makes_a_coach_2-07.pdf.

3. Robert E. Logan and Tara Miller, *From Followers to Leaders* (St. Charles, IL: ChurchSmart Resources, 2007), 35.

Chapter 4

1. "New Life Fellowship Church," 2017. Accessed February 20, 2017, http://newlifefellowship.org/about-us/about-new-life/new-lifes-history/#headline1.

2. Peter Scazzero, "The Emotionally Healthy Church Planter," 2012. Accessed February 20, 2017, http://www.emotionallyhealthy.org/wp-content/uploads/2015/07/EHChurchPlanter.pdf.

3. Steve Addison, "The Startup Guide to Coaching Leaders," 2002, 18. Accessed February 20, 2017, http://sojourner.typepad.com/files/coaching_leaders_startup_guide_steve_addison-1.pdf.

4. Peter Scazzero, *Emotionally Healthy Spirituality: Unleash a Revolution in Your Life in Christ* (Nashville, TN: Thomas Nelson Publishers, 2006), 37.

Part Two

1. Steven L. Ogne and Tim Roehl, *TransforMissional Coaching: Empowering Spiritual Leaders in a Changing Ministry World* (Nashville, TN: B&H Publishing Group, 2008).

2. Robert E. Logan, Sherilyn Carlton, and Tara Miller, *Coaching 101: Discover the Power of Coaching* (n.p.: Churchsmart Resources, 2003), 26.

3. Tony Stoltzfus, "What Makes a Coach?" 2006. Accessed February 28, 2017, http://coach22.com/discover-coaching/resources/what_makes_a_coach_2-07.pdf.

Chapter 5

1. Rick Warren, *The Purpose Driven Life: What on Earth Am I Here For?* (Grand Rapids, MI: Zondervan, 2012), 23.

2. Keith E. Webb, *The COACH Model® for Christian Leaders: Powerful Leadership Skills for Solving Problems, Reaching Goals, and Developing Others* (Bellevue, WA: Active Results LLC, 2012), 19–24. The COACH Model® is the registered trademark of Keith E. Webb. Used by permission, http://keithwebb.com.

3. Ibid.

Chapter 6

1. Mac Lake, *Multiply Church Planter Training*, Trainer's ed., 163.
2. Ibid. 162–63.

Chapter 7

1. Martin B. Copenhaver, *Jesus Is the Question: The 307 Questions Jesus Asked and the 3 He Answered* (Nashville, TN: Abingdon Press, 2014), Kindle ed., Location 182.
2. John Whitmore, *Coaching for Performance: Growing People, Performance, and Purpose* (Boston, MA: Nicholas Brealey Publishing, 2002), 49.
3. Steve Nicolson and Jeff Bailey, *Coaching Church Planters* (Anaheim, CA: Association of Vineyard Churches USA, 2001), 41.

Chapter 8

1. "Fanatic." Accessed February 22, 2017, http://www.dictionary.com/browse/fanatic.
2. John C. Maxwell, *Good Leaders Ask Great Questions: Your Foundation for Successful Leadership* (New York, NY: Center Street Publishers, 2014), 37.
3. Ibid., 31.

Chapter 9

1. Heather, Bond, "5 Reasons Why I Want My Husband to Have a Coach: Coaching Reflections from a Church Planting Wife." *CNBC Horizon* 29, no. 3 (June 2016): 17. Excerpts taken from this article.
2. Wayne Cordeiro, *Leading on Empty: Refilling Your Tank and Renewing Your Passion* (Minneapolis, MN: Bethany House, 2009), 13.
3. *Seek God for the City 2017: Prayers of Biblical Hope*, 22nd ed. (Austin, TX: WayMakers, 2017), 44. Used with permission.
4. Paul David Tripp, *Dangerous Calling: Confronting the Unique Challenges of Pastoral Ministry* (Wheaton, IL: Crossway, 2012), 84.
5. Peter Scazzero, "The Emotionally Healthy Church Planter," 2012. Accessed February 19, 2017, http://www.emotionallyhealthy.org/wp-content/uploads/2015/07/EHChurchPlanter.pdf.

Chapter 10

1. Susan Scott, *Fierce Conversations: Achieving Success at Work and in Life, One Conversation at a Time* (New York, NY: Berkley Books, 2004), xv.

2. Jeff Christopherson, *Kingdom Matrix: Designing a Church for the Kingdom of God*, Expanded ed. (Boise, ID: Elevate Publishing, 2012), 37.

3. Steve Ogne and Tim Roehl, *TransforMissional Coaching: Empowering Leaders in a Changing Ministry World* (Nashville, TN: B&H Publishing Group, 2008), 69.

4. G. T. Doran, "There's a S.M.A.R.T. Way to Write Management's Goals and Objectives," *Management Review (AMA FORUM)* 70, no. 11 (1981): 35–36.

5. Keith E. Webb, *The COACH Model® for Christian Leaders: Powerful Leadership Skills for Solving Problems, Reaching Goals, and Developing Others* (Bellevue, WA: Active Results LLC, 2012), 96. The COACH Model® is the registered trademark of Keith E. Webb. Used by permission, http://keithwebb.com.

Chapter 11

1. Meredith Yackle, "Coaching: Send Network Multiplies Communities of Healthy Church Planters," *On Mission* 19, no. 3 (2016): 10–14. Excerpts taken from this article.

2. Paul David Tripp, *Dangerous Calling: Confronting the Unique Challenges of Pastoral Ministry* (Wheaton, IL: Crossway, 2012), 206.

3. Ed Cerny, *Notes from the Coach: The Power of the Pro-Vision™ Life* (Conway, SC: Coach's Corner Press, 1997), 7.

Chapter 12

1. Dhati Lewis, *Among Wolves: Disciple-Making in the City* (Nashville, TN: B&H Publishing Group, 2017), 47.

2. Gary Smalley and John Trent, *The Keys to Growing in Love: The Language of Love; Love Is a Decision; The Two Sides of Love* (New York, NY: Inspirational, 1996), 430–84.

3. Jeff Christopherson, *Kingdom Matrix: Designing a Church for the Kingdom of God*, Expanded ed. (Boise, ID: Elevate Publishing, 2012), 215.

4. Robert Hargrove, *Masterful Coaching*, 3rd ed. (San Francisco, CA: Jossey-Bass, 2008), 129.

Chapter 13

1. Ron Shepard, *Seattle Send City Missionary Internal Document*.
2. Ed Stetzer and Daniel Im, *Planting Missional Churches: Your Guide to Starting Churches that Multiply*, 2nd ed. (Nashville, TN: B&H Academic, 2016), 38.
3. Tony Stoltzfus, "Coaching Weaknesses." Accessed February 23, 2017, http://www.coach22.com/coaching-weaknesses/.

Chapter 14

1. Joe Bulger, DDS, "Top 10 Reasons People HATE Dentists." Accessed January 06, 2017, http://www.hatedentists.com/1363/top-10-reasons-people-hate-dentists/.
2. "Cultivate Church." Accessed February 24, 2017, http://cultivatenj.com/.
3. Martin B. Copenhaver, *Jesus Is the Question: The 307 Questions Jesus Asked and the 3 He Answered* (Nashville, TN: Abingdon Press, 2014), Kindle ed., Location 308.
4. "Milquetoast." Accessed February 26, 2017. http://www.urbandictionary.com/define.php?term=milquetoast.

Part Three

1. "Making the DXP." Accessed December 10, 2016, http://www.dominosdxp.com/.
2. J. Robert Clinton, *The Making of a Leader: Recognizing the Lessons and Stages of Leadership Development* (Colorado Springs, CO: NavPress, 2012), 39–40.

Chapter 15

1. ChartsBin, "Most Popular Sports by Country," 2015. Accessed February 18, 2017, http://chartsbin.com/view/33104.
2. Gary Belsky and Neil Fine, *On the Origin of Sports: The Early History and Original Rules of Everybody's Favorite Games* (New York: Artisan, 2016), 9.
3. Ibid., 76.

4. Ibid.

5. Paul David Tripp, *Dangerous Calling: Confronting the Unique Challenges of Pastoral* Ministry (Wheaton, IL: Crossway, 2012), 77.

6. Steve Addison, "The Startup Guide to Coaching Leaders," 2002. Accessed February 20, 2017, http://sojourner.typepad.com/files/coaching_leaders_startup_guide_steve_addison-1.pdf.

Chapter 16

1. "The Space Race," 2010. Accessed December 27, 2016, http://www.history.com/topics/space-race.

2. "Encore: Astronaut John Glenn Recalls Historic Orbit Of Earth," 2016. Accessed February 21, 2017, http://www.npr.org/2016/12/09/505012157/encore-astronaut-john-glenn-recalls-historic-orbit-of-earth.

3. Pat Hood, *The Sending Church: The Church Must Leave the Building* (Nashville, TN: B&H Publishing Group, 2013), 234.

4. Ed Stetzer and Daniel Im, *Planting Missional Churches: Your Guide to Starting Churches that Multiply*, 2nd ed. (Nashville, TN: B&H Academic, 2016), 322.

Chapter 17

1. Ed Cerny, *Notes from the Coach: The Power of the Pro-Vision™ Life* (Conway, SC: Coach's Corner Press, 1997), 23–29.

2. Simon Sinek, *Begin with the Why: How Great Leaders Inspire Everyone to Take Action* (New York, NY: Portfolio/Penguin, 2009), 42.

Chapter 18

1. "Allen Iverson." Accessed December 16, 2016, http://www.hoophall.com/hall-of-famers/allen-iverson.

2. "Allen Iverson 'PRACTICE?!'" 2013. Accessed December 16, 2016, https://www.youtube.com/watch?v=Y_yNPjMjbmk.

3. Keith E. Webb, *The COACH Model® for Christian Leaders: Powerful Leadership Skills for Solving Problems, Reaching Goals, and Developing* Others (Bellevue, WA: Active Results LLC, 2012), 153. The COACH Model® is the registered trademark of Keith E. Webb. Used by permission, http://keithwebb.com.

4. Mark Clifton, *Reclaiming Glory: Revitalizing Dying Churches* (Nashville, TN: B&H Publishing Group, 2016), 74.

5. Keith E. Webb, "How to Get 300% Greater Training Results." Accessed February 22, 2017, http://keithwebb.com/get-300-greater-training-results/.

Appendix E

1. Pat Hood, *The Sending Church: The Church Must Leave the Building* (Nashville, TN: B&H Publishing Group, 2013), 220.

Appendix F

1. Clint Clifton, *Church Planting Thresholds: A Gospel-Centered Guide* (New City Network, 2016), 180–82.